THE LITTLE BOOK OF
QUEENS PARK RANGERS

Written by David Clayton

THE LITTLE BOOK Of
QUEENS PARK RANGERS

This edition first published in the UK in 2008
By Green Umbrella Publishing

© Green Umbrella Publishing 2008

www.gupublishing.co.uk

Publishers Jules Gammond and Vanessa Gardner

Printed and bound in Poland

ISBN 978-1906635-23-7

Contents

Ainsworth, Gareth
(2003 – onwards)

IF YOU LIKE WATCHING NO-HOLDS barred, all-action type footballers, Gareth Ainsworth is the player for you. One of the Hoops' best signings in recent times, Ainsworth arrived on a free transfer from Cardiff City in June 2003 after a nomadic career spent mostly in the lower leagues. He began life with non-League Northwich Victoria before being snapped up by Preston North End in 1991 as a raw teenager. He would spend five years with the Lilywhites – punctuated by an ill-fated four-month spell at Cambridge United – before moving to Lincoln City for £25,000 in 1995. He became something of a legend while at Sincil Bank and averaged almost a goal every other game during his two-year spell – a

record that convinced Port Vale to splash out £500,000 for his services.

He continued to blossom while at Vale and won a dream move to the Premiership when Wimbledon paid £2m for the attacking wide-man, yet his platform on the big stage was ruined by injury and he never really had a decent run with the Dons. Known as "Wild Thing" during his five-year stay, he was loaned out to Preston and Walsall before he signed for Cardiff City for a nominal fee in 2003. He played just nine games for the Bluebirds before Ian Holloway brought him to QPR three months later.

It was as if Ainsworth had found his spiritual home and he began his career at Loftus Road in spectacular style, scoring

twice against Blackpool on his debut and added two more fantastic strikes against Rushden & Diamonds – one of them was voted ITV's Goal of the Season.

Injury forced him to miss much of the campaign, though he returned to fitness in time to help QPR win promotion and since then he has etched his name into club folklore as a firm favourite with the supporters.

Whether he's flying down the wing or crunching into tackles, Ainsworth doesn't seem capable of giving less than 100 per cent effort and his move towards a coaching role with the Hoops began when former manager Luigi De Canio briefly employed him as one of his assistants. New boss Iain Dowie then offered him the position of player-coach during the summer of 2008, ensuring he remains a vital part of QPR FC for the foreseeable future.

LEFT Gareth Ainsworth in action against West Bromwich Albion

Allen Family

NO FAMILY HAS CONTRIBUTED more to Queen's Park Rangers Football Club than the Allens; Les, Clive, Martin and Bradley. All four men enjoyed significant careers at Loftus Road and it all began with Les Allen who joined QPR in 1965 from Tottenham who had just signed Jimmy Greaves.

It was something of a shock move, with Spurs one of the country's biggest teams at the time and QPR marooned in the Third Division, but Allen was confident he'd made the right move – partly after chairman Jim Gregory had assured him his club were moving in the right direction and would be a top-flight team before too long.

Allen was a cultured forward who was initially dismayed with the kick and rush tactics his new team employed, but gradually, Les and other experienced players such as Jim Langley got the younger members of the side passing the ball around and the style and panache QPR fans yearned for became engrained with the club's psyche from then on.

The crowds began to increase – doubling then tripling – and Allen was hugely influential. In Allen's second season, QPR announced their arrival on the football map by winning the League Cup with a dramatic 3-2 win over West Bromwich Albion and winning promotion to the Second Division and then the First Division.

Allen decided to retire at the end of the 1968/69 season and he combined playing with managing during the last few months of the campaign, succeeding Tommy Docherty, though relegation was merely a formality by that point. He then left Rangers to become a scout at Swindon Town having scored 55 goals in 128 appearances for QPR – a fantastic return from a wonderful player.

Of course, his association with the club doesn't end there and Les' son Clive joined the QPR youth set-up in the mid-seventies, making his debut against Coventry City in 1978. He scored a hat-trick in a 5-1 win – what a way to announce your arrival in senior football! Though Rangers were relegated at the end of his first season, during his first full campaign in 1978/79, Clive scored 28 goals, alerting Arsenal who successfully bid £1.25m for the teenage hot-shot. He would spend less than two months with the Gunners, never playing a competitive game before being sold on to Crystal Palace in one of the most bizarre transfer stories of that or any year.

Clive returned to Loftus Road in 1981 when Terry Venables was manager and it was his goals that helped Second Division QPR to a first ever FA Cup final, ironically against his father Les' former team Spurs. Clive was injured after just two minutes of the final and though he lasted until just after the break, he was forced to come off and missed the subsequent replay a few days later.

His goals helped the Hoops to promotion in 1982/83 and he was again productive in a ninth-placed finish in the top-flight the following year. He won his first England cap while still a QPR player

RIGHT Bradley Allen

before finally severing ties with the club in 1984 by following in father Les' footsteps, signing for Spurs. His record of 83 goals in 158 games while at Loftus Road is nothing short of incredible.

Clive's cousin Martin Allen then took on the family mantle, making his debut in October 1984 after coming through the club's youth ranks. A rugged, tough-tackling midfielder, Martin won England youth and Under-21 honours during his five years with the Hoops before joining West Ham in September 1989 for £550,000 during which time he'd played 167 times for the R's, scoring 19 goals.

Clive Allen's younger brother Bradley, who joined QPR as a youngster, had already made his debut by the time cousin Martin had left. Though a different type of striker to Clive, Bradley was a more industrious, skilful player – though less prolific – and he served the club with great pride over a seven-year period, scoring 32 goals in 94 appearances before joining Charlton Athletic in 1996.

RIGHT Bradley Allen

Ardiles, Osvaldo

(1988 – 89)

THOUGH HE WAS AT THE END OF an illustrious playing career and he only made eight appearances for QPR all told, Osvaldo Ardiles remains one of the biggest names in world football to have played for the club.

The Argentinean star rose to fame during his country's 1978 World Cup triumph and after the tournament, both he and Ricky Villa joined Tottenham, where they became huge crowd favourites in the process.

The 1982 Falklands War between Britain and Argentina made life difficult for Ardiles, who was loaned out to various foreign clubs while the conflict raged and between 1982 and 1985, Ardiles, in his prime, played just 20 times for Spurs.

A broken leg didn't help either and he never really recaptured the magic that had made him an international superstar, going out on loan to Blackburn Rovers in 1988 before manager Jim Smith brought Ossie to Loftus Road on a free transfer in August 1988.

Now 36, Ossie made just four starts, coming on four times as sub and though his brain was sharp and his skill occasionally apparent, he was a pale shadow of the diminutive midfielder of the early eighties and he left on a free transfer to Swindon Town 11 months later.

LEFT Ossie Ardiles

Player stats:	
Apps	4 + 4 sub
Goals	0

Bannister, Gary
(1984 – 98)

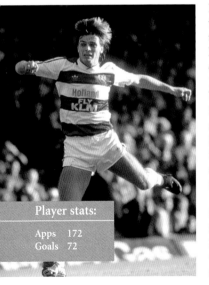

Player stats:

Apps 172
Goals 72

IT WAS GOING TO take something special to fill the sizeable hole left by Clive Allen's departure during the 1984 close season but somehow, Gary Bannister managed it and quickly established himself as a firm crowd favourite at Loftus Road in the process.

Alan Mullery paid Sheffield Wednesday £200,000 for the 24-year-old Bannister who made his home debut just 12 days later during a 3-1 win over West Brom. He scored his first goal three days after that and settled in to his new surrounds quickly thereafter. Bannister seemed to revel on Loftus Road's plastic artificial pitch with 17 of his 28 goals coming during home games – five more were also classed as "home goals", though they came during two UEFA Cup home legs played at Highbury, making his home ratio even more impressive. Bannister played in all 55 games the R's played in 1984/85 and his haul of 18 goals the following season proved what a tremendous acquisition he was. He added 16 the season after that and another 10 in his final year before moving to Coventry City.

Bardsley, David

(1989 – 98)

ONE OF THE BEST CLUB SERVANTS of modern times, David Bardsley played for QPR for almost a decade and went on to win two England caps while at Loftus Road. Signed from Oxford

United for £500,000, Bardsley began his career with the Hoops as a wide midfielder, but struggled in his first few months and soon became a target for the notorious boo boys. Manager Trevor Francis played him at right-back for a couple of games and he did fairly well, but few believed he would last more than a season before being shipped on. When new boss Don Howe took over, however, Bardsley began to look more composed in his new role and soon it seemed as though he'd always played in defence. By the end of his second season, he was an integral member of the QPR side and never really looked back. He struck up a fine understanding with Les Ferdinand and Bardsley's overlapping runs down the right produced a number of crosses that Ferdinand tucked away.

During the 1992/93 campaign, with Bardsley by that time recognised as one of the best right-backs in the country, he won two England caps. His later years with Rangers were, however, blighted by injury. Though he left on a free transfer to Blackpool in 1998, he is still thought of as one of the best right-backs since Dave Clement – high praise indeed.

Player stats:

Apps	255 + 1 sub
Goals	6

FAR LEFT Gary Bannister

LEFT David Bardsley in action during a 1995 match against Millwall

Barker, Simon

(1988 – 98)

WHEN QPR BOSS JIM SMITH PAID a club record of £400,000 for Blackburn Rovers' 24-year-old midfielder Simon Barker, it's fair to say one or two eyebrows were raised. But the transfer fee, in hindsight, represented fantastic business by Smith as Barker went on to patrol the Hoops' midfield for a decade. The tough-tackling ball-winner soon became a crowd favourite, chiefly because Barker never gave less than 100 per cent every time he pulled on a QPR shirt and with not far short of 400 appearances during those 10 years at Loftus Road, he rarely missed a game, either. His versatility was evident in his first season too and during a time when the only shirt numbers you'd see during a match were numbered 1 to 12, Barker wore all but four team numbers as he played in most positions for the club, though he would eventually make the No. 8 jersey his own. He won four England Under-21 caps during his career (all while with Blackburn), but was never given the opportunity of winning a full cap for his country.

He was awarded a benefit match against Jamaica in 1998 shortly before he joined Port Vale. Barker today is a senior executive of the PFA.

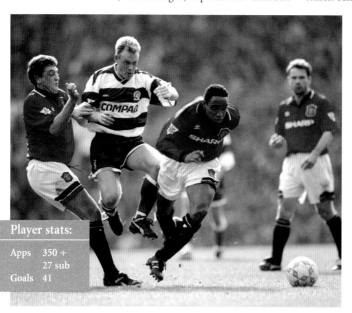

BELOW Simon Barker takes on Steve Bruce and Paul Ince of Manchester United

Player stats:

Apps	350 + 27 sub
Goals	41

Bedford, Brian

(1959 – 1965)

FEW QPR STRIKERS HAVE STRUCK fear onto opposing defenders in quite the same manner as predator supreme Brian Bedford who notched up an astonishing 161 goals in 258 appearances during his time at Loftus Road. It

was Alec Stock who identified Bedford's talent and he was more than happy to pay Bournemouth the princely sum of £750. Bedford more than repaid that faith as he banged in 27 goals during his first campaign with the Hoops. He followed that with 37 in 48 starts during the 1960/61 season and went two better by scoring 39 in his third season! Two 23-goal hauls in the league during seasons 1963/64 and 1964/65 wrote the Welsh forward's name into the club's history books before joining Scunthorpe United in

1965 and drifting out of league football completely two years later. Bedford became a professional tennis coach after retiring from the game, though did return to Loftus Road in the capacity of stadium manager during the 1990s. A true Rangers legend, Bedford's name is up there with the likes of Les Allen, George Goddard and Clive Allen – what price his talent today?

Player stats:

Apps	258
Goals	161

BELOW Brian Bedford is seated left on the front row of this team line-up

Bircham, Marc

(2002 – 07)

RIGHT Marc Bircham battles with Youssef Safri of Norwich for possession of the ball

MARC BIRCHAM HAS TO BE ONE of the most colourful characters to have played for QPR over the years – literally. The tough-tackling midfielder joined from Millwall in 2002 after being snapped up by manager Ian Holloway on a free transfer and for his home debut against Chesterfield he ran out with his hair dyed blue and white! Bircham, a huge boyhood fan of the R's, soon became a cult figure among the supporters and he never disappointed either with his all-action displays or with his variety of different hairstyles and colours throughout the 2002/03 campaign. He played in the play-off final at the end of that season when the R's lost to Cardiff City, but a year later he was celebrating after Holloway's side won promotion back to the Championship. When Holloway left in 2006, Bircham was placed on the transfer list by new boss, Gary Waddock, but refused to quit the club he loved. With a year left on his contract, he worked harder than ever, won his place back in the team and was handed the captaincy after which he responded by playing the best football of his career. He also won 17 caps for Canada, several during his time at Loftus Road. In 2007 he reluctantly left QPR, signing for Yeovil Town on a Bosman.

Bowles, Stan

(1972 – 79)

STAN BOWLES WROTE HIMSELF into QPR folklore by doing the seemingly impossible and helping supporters forget about another mercurial striker, Rodney Marsh. Bowles and QPR were a match made in heaven and throughout the mid-seventies, Super Stan proved that he was capable of not only surviving in the top-flight, he excelled.

There was no small amount of irony that Marsh joined Manchester City – the very club that had sacked Bowles a couple of years earlier due to disciplinary problems off the pitch. After brief spells with Bury and Crewe, Bowles moved to Carlisle United and began to restore his reputation as a forward with plenty of potential.

Bowles was a law unto himself and when asked how he felt about signing for QPR and taking on the coveted No.10 jersey from Marsh, Bowles claimed he'd never heard of him!

Rangers paid Carlisle £112,000 for Bowles' services – most of the money the club had received from the sale of Marsh – but it soon proved to be money

LEFT Stan Bowles

extremely well spent.

On his home debut against Nottingham Forest, Bowles scored one of the goals in a 3-0 victory. His skill, vision and technique were perfectly suited to a QPR side with a reputation for playing silky football and he found the net eight times in his first 13 games. At Sunderland on the last day of the 1972/73 season, the hosts paraded the

FA Cup in front of a rapturous Roker Park full-house – Stan's response? He kicked the ball at the cup, knocking it into the air and then scored twice in a 3-0 win, ending the campaign as second top scorer to Don Givens with 18 in 39 starts as the R's won promotion to Division One.

The following season Bowles played every game of Rangers' season, scoring 23 goals in 51 appearances, proving his worth beyond all doubt and forging a love affair with the Loftus Road fans that would render him virtually untouchable. He reached double figures in each of the next two campaigns, yet he was criminally ignored by England time and time again.

During the 1976/77 season, Bowles broke all existing UEFA Cup records in England by bagging 11 goals in just eight games, but that was his last truly effective campaign and by the start of 1979/80, he'd even relinquished the No.10 shirt with Tony Currie eventually taking over the prized jersey. His final game for Rangers was during a 2-2 draw away to Wrexham in November 1979 before a surprise – and ill-fated – move to Brian Clough's Nottingham Forest. The fans have never forgotten one of their favourite sons, however, and in 2004 he was voted the greatest QPR player ever.

BELOW The mercurial Stan Bowles

Briatore, Flavio

MULTI-MILLIONAIRE ITALIAN BUSI-nessman Flavio Briatore couldn't have been much further away from owning a football club than he was just a decade ago. A former travelling insurance sales-man, Briatore moved into the stock market, eventually becoming close friends with Luciano Benetton, founder of the world famous Benetton clothing company. Briatore and Benetton became business partners and Briatore made his fortune when Benetton exploded in the USA and he remained head of the US operations before becoming Commercial Director and then Managing Director of Benetton's Formula One team. He later switched to Renault and during his time in the sport he signed up Michael Schumacher and discovered Fernando Alonso – both of whom became World F1 Champions. Today he manages F1 drivers Heikki Kovalainen and Mark Webber. Briatore became close friends with F1 supremo Bernie Ecclestone and together the pair purchased QPR in September 2007. In December of the same year they were joined by Lakshmi Mittal, the fourth

ABOVE Flavio Briatore signs autographs for fans

richest man on the planet to form the wealthiest club ownership in the world. Together they plan to turn the R's into a major Premier League outfit; they plan to do this gradually rather than pump-ing limitless funds. Owner of fashion labels, high class restaurants and exclu-sive nightclubs, Briatore has now added football to his passion for fast cars and fashion. He is married to the beautiful Elisabetta Gregoraci and the driver of the bridal car? Fernando Alonso!

Buzsaky, Akos

(2007 – onwards)

RIGHT Glenn Whelan of Stoke City challenges Akos Buzsaky, 2008

OFTEN IT'S THE SUPPORTERS OF the club a player leaves who give a clue to how highly-rated he was prior to his move to pastures new and that can be said of Hungarian winger Akos Buzsaky. When he was allowed to join QPR on loan in October 2007, Plymouth Argyle supporters were up in arms about their hero's departure.

Buzsaky, once signed by then Porto manager Jose Mourinho, soon showed Hoops fans why the Pilgrims' followers were so upset at losing their prized asset as he settled in immediately to his new surrounds at Loftus Road scoring six goals in a dozen games. QPR fans were not interested in if Buzsaky would sign permanently, just when, and by public demand, he joined the club on January 2 2008 for a bargain fee believed to be in the region of £500,000.

Buzsaky was a key member of the Rangers side that impressed in the second half of the 2007/08 campaign and his spectacular goal against Blackpool – one of 10 in 27 appearances – was voted Goal of the Season by Hoops fans. Now

Buzsaky has taken on the coveted No.10 jersey, great things are expected of him over the next few years – don't bet against him delivering – and he will be an integral member of Iain Dowie's team as QPR attempt to return to top-flight football in season 2008/09.

Camp, Lee
(2004 & 2007 – onwards)

FORMER ENGLAND UNDER-21 goalkeeper Lee Camp's move to Loftus Road developed over a three-year period before he finally put pen to paper on a permanent deal in July 2007. He initially arrived on loan from Derby County in 2004, returning to Pride Park after a short – though hugely impressive – spell with the Hoops, who won promotion that season. With first team opportunities limited with the Rams, in February 2007, the talented keeper jumped at the opportunity to return to QPR on a temporary basis and his form and consistency during his second spell were rewarded with a permanent deal with the R's paying Derby £300,000 for his services. Camp won a total of five caps for the England Under-21s –

including a first professional game at the new Wembley Stadium – and was the only QPR player to start every game during his first full season. He was voted runner-up in the club's 2007/08 Player of the Year award, confirming his popularity among the Rangers faithful. In today's world of inflated transfer fees, the talented young keeper represents excellent value and Iain Dowie will be hoping Camp proves to be the rock in his defence as the R's attempt to win promotion to the Premier League.

Player stats:

Apps	69

BELOW Lee Camp, 2008

Celebrity Fans

RIGHT Martin Clunes

BELOW Shane Ritchie

BELOW RIGHT Ade Edmondson

POP STARS, SPORTSMEN, FOOT-ballers, comedians and celebrity chefs – just a few of the occupations held by celebrity QPR fans. One of the highest profile Super Hoops fans must be the

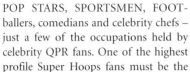

Naked Chef himself, Jamie Oliver – so far Jamie has not complained about the catering at Loftus Road so the pies mustn't be too bad! Former Eastenders star Shane Ritchie, former Young Ones star Ade Edmondson and Men Behaving Badly star Martin Clunes are all Loft regulars while a few of the music world's bad boys – Nick Cave, Pete Docherty from Babyshambles, Glen Matlock from The Sex Pistols and Mick Jones of The Clash – are Rangers die-hards – as is former Wham! star Andrew Ridgeley. Former Transvision Vamp lead singer Wendy James is a Rangers fan as is Phil

Collins who can't take in as many games as he did in his younger years. Cricketers Ashley Giles and Alex Tudor get along whenever they can and former QPR idol Rodney Marsh has never forgotten the club that gave him a start in league football. Dennis Wise is a Hoops fan, rather than Chelsea, and cult comic Bill Bailey has been known to mention his beloved R's during his live routine.

Clement, Dave

(1965 – 1979)

A QPR LEGEND, DAVE CLEMENT'S story is one of pride, triumph and ultimately, tragedy. A product of the club's youth policy, Clement's eye-catching displays at right-back soon won him England Youth recognition and after signing professional forms in 1965 he made his league debut during a 5-1 win at home to Scunthorpe United in April 1967 – just a month after the Hoops had won the League Cup – on their way to promotion from Division Three. The following campaign, the teenage Clement established himself as first

Player stats:

Apps	472 + 4 sub
Goals	28

BELOW Dave Clement tracks Kevin Keegan of Liverpool

he managed five goals from defence. He missed just three league games between August 1970 and April 1974; he was among the most consistent full-backs in England – confirmed by the five caps he won for his country during that time, though his first cap didn't come until 1976 against Wales. Though he was a regular first team member during the latter half of the seventies, he rarely averaged more than 30 appearances a season during that time.

After the Hoops were relegated at the end of the 1978/79 campaign, Rangers accepted Bolton Wanderers' bid of £170,000 for Clement, bringing an end to a 14-year association with QPR during which time he served the club with great distinction. Just three years later, following a broken leg and a bout of severe depression, Clement committed suicide. He still had such a lot to offer football and he will never be forgotten by QPR supporters.

team regular, gradually making the No.2 jersey his own as the R's won back-to-back promotion. His first goal for the club came against Tottenham in January 1969 and during the 1969/70 campaign

Crouch, Peter

(2000 – 01)

PETER CROUCH IS UNDOUBTEDLY one of the highest profile players to have played for QPR in recent years – though only retrospectively speaking. Teenager Crouch was a lanky giant of a striker who seemed to have little hope of progressing into the first team at White Hart Lane and had a couple of low-profile loan spells outside the top four English leagues with little success. With Gerry Francis back at Loftus Road for a second spell as manager, he reckoned Crouch might be worth a gamble on and in July 2000, Rangers agreed a £60,000 fee with Spurs and Crouch made the short journey across London where his career would begin in earnest.

QPR fans didn't know what to make of the 6' 7" beanpole, but he soon won them over with his intelligent hold-up play and excellent ability on the ground. By the end of his first season, a host of clubs were on Crouch's trail and though he only scored 10 goals in 42 appearances, he provided assists for many of his team-mates. He was the ideal target man, plus a lot more and though QPR were relegated at the end of that first campaign, Crouch had done enough to see his value rocket and the cash-strapped Hoops were thankful when Portsmouth bid £1.25m in July 2001 to secure his services – cash that helped the club keep afloat and for that reason Crouch will always be thought of fondly by Rangers supporters.

Player stats:

Apps	42
Goals	10

BELOW Peter Crouch, 2000

Currie, Tony

(1979 – 1982)

BELOW RIGHT Tony Currie, 1980

FAR RIGHT Currie's silky skills were well suited to the Hoops' plastic pitch

THERE WAS NO LITTLE SIGNIFI-cance that Tony Currie wore the No.10 jersey on his QPR debut at home to Fulham – the former Sheffield United and Leeds United play-maker possessed all the necessary attributes needed to wear the coveted shirt and that he was given it for his first game – in which he scored – was a statement of intent rather than a coincidence. Currie spent the majority of the seventies at the top of most opposing fans' wish-list and he won 19 England caps during that time. His superb technical abil-ity, silky skills and vision made him an instant hit at Loftus Road, yet he could have been a QPR player for almost a decade by the time he actually did sign – Currie had been on the Hoops' books as a youngster – but wasn't offered a contract!

With Stan Bowles' career winding down, Currie was the perfect man to take on the creativity mantle and when Bowles left for Nottingham Forest in December 1979, Currie became the club's resident No.10.

Currie was never less than a delight to watch and he won a legion of admirers over the next couple of seasons, though injury kept him out of part of his sec-ond campaign with the Hoops and much of his third and final season, by which time he'd handed the No.10 shirt over to the new creative outlet – Simon Stainrod – in time-honoured fashion. Currie was to bow out of his QPR career at the top, however, he captained the team in the FA Cup final replay against Tottenham. He dropped out of the game through injury in 1982, but returned with Southend United and several other lower league clubs (though only played a handful of matches), before embarking on a spell at non-League level.

Dowie, Iain
(1998 – 2001) &
Head Coach (2008 – onwards)

Player stats:

Apps 31
Goals 2

ABOVE Iain Dowie gives instructions via mobile phone

NORTHERN IRELAND INTERNA-tional Iain Dowie took his first steps into management with QPR, so it is perhaps fitting that he has now returned to take charge of the most ambitious club outside the Premier League. Dowie's playing career began at non-League level before he was signed by Luton Town, Southampton and West Ham – the club he left to join the Hoops in 1998. With his career winding down, he signed for the R's and played much of his time in central defence before he took on the role of player-manager for QPR reserves. Dowie was briefly in charge of the first team in a caretaker capacity after Ray Harford was dismissed and prior to Gerry Francis' appointment. He remained at Loftus Road until 2001 after which he pursued his own management career, initially with Oldham Athletic before having spells at several clubs, including Crystal Palace, Charlton Athletic and Coventry City. Following Luigi de Canio's departure in 2008, it was Dowie the club appointed as head coach – and backed with a healthy transfer budget and a strong squad, Dowie has been given perhaps the greatest opportunity of his career so far. He has promised to do it "his way".

Europe

THOUGH QPR HAVE ONLY QUALI-fied for Europe on two occasions, each UEFA Cup run left lasting memories. The first time the Hoops entered the UEFA Cup was in 1976 – a reward for a best-ever finish in the top-flight of second – with SK Brann of Norway their first round oppo-nents. A classy Rangers side bided their time during the first leg at Loftus Road, but once Stan Bowles opened the scoring on 29 minutes, the Norwegians never stood a chance, particularly as Bowles seemed to have some kind of personal vendetta against them and had completed his hat-trick with little more than an hour played. Don Masson's late fourth meant that the second leg was little more than a for-mality and Bowles again tore Brann's defence apart, scoring another hat-trick in a 7-0 romp.

Dave Sexton's men were in confident mood when they travelled to Czechoslovakia for their second round

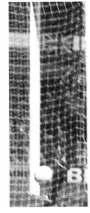

BELOW Cologne keeper Harold Schumacher is helpless as Dave Webb scores for QPR

clash with Slovan Bratislava and Bowles was again in electric form, scoring twice before the break to give his team a 2-1 lead, though the hosts fought back to draw 3-3 in a hugely entertaining match. The return was just as thrilling, with QPR in devastating form winning 5-2 with Don Givens helping himself to a hat-trick on this occasion.

People began to wonder – could this little-known English side really go all the way? Nineteen goals in four games suggested they could be the dark horses for the UEFA Cup that season – and following a third round clash at Loftus Road against German side Cologne, it seemed as though European football and QPR were a match made in heaven. Don Givens, Dave Webb and Bowles gave the Hoops a 3-0 first leg lead against a very good Bundesliga side, but the second leg proved something of a reality check for Sexton's side. The key moment of that game was Don Masson's early goal, giving the R's a 4-0 aggregate lead and the timing was perfect as Cologne roared back with a vengeance, winning the game 4-1, but going out thanks to Masson's priceless strike.

Now into the quarter-finals, whoever QPR drew it was going to be a tough match – and so it proved. Interest among Rangers fans was at fever pitch and the club wanted to switch the game to Wembley, but their Greek opponents AEK Athens objected to a one-day delay if the venue was switched. They probably wished they had, though, after a 3-0 defeat at Loftus Road thanks to two

Gerry Francis penalties and another from Bowles – surely a solid second leg display would see Rangers into the semi-finals? Sadly, inexperience of continental opposition showed as an injury hit QPR struggled to contain the Greeks and AEK forced extra time with a 3-0 scoreline no more than they deserved. Neither side could find the net in extra time and AEK eventually progressed after a penalty shoot-out.

Rangers have never played a European tie since the match against AEK in 1977, because the next time they entered the UEFA Cup in 1984/85, the plastic pitch at Loftus Road – banned in European competition by UEFA - meant the Hoops had to play their home times at Arsenal's Highbury stadium. Icelandic side KR Reykjavik were put to the sword first, 3-0 on their own ground and 4-0 at Highbury, with Gary Bannister helping himself to a hat-trick

in the second leg.

Yugoslavian side Partizan Belgrade were next up and were anticipated to be much tougher opponents than the previous round – and Partizan appeared to be on their way to a victory at Highbury as they took a 2-1 lead in the first half. QPR again had a taste for European football, however, and during a magical performance, they destroyed the Yugoslav's after the break, winning 6-2 and appeared to have killed the tie off. Unfortunately, Partizan were far from finished.

Under the cosh from the word go, Rangers were just 1-0 down moments from the break – yet within two minutes of the re-start, Partizan had scored twice to lead 3-0. The next goal would prove to be crucial – if QPR scored, the balance would tilt back their way, if the hosts scored, they would go through if there was no further scoring. Sadly, it was the latter scenario that transpired, with Partizan grabbing a fourth on 65 minutes to win the tie on away goals.

Twice QPR had taken healthy leads into the second leg and twice they'd been knocked out though each run had resulted in goals, individual brilliance and drama.

FA Cup

THERE IS ONLY ONE season that Rangers really threatened to lift the FA Cup and that was during the 1981/82 campaign when the club went all the way to the final as a Division Two side. The journey to Wembley began when the R's were drawn at home to First Division Middlesbrough in the third round. The visitors took a first half lead but Simon Stainrod secured a replay with a 70th minute equaliser. Freezing conditions meant the game at Ayresome Park was aborted several times before eventually taking place just five days before the fourth round was due to take place. In an exciting game, Rangers led 2-0 through a Stainrod brace, but the hosts fought back to force extra time with Warren Neill heading a 117th

minute winner for Terry Venables' side. A replay was again needed to see off plucky Fourth Division Blackpool in the fourth round, but following a 0-0 draw at Bloomfield Road, Clive Allen destroyed the Seasiders with four goals during a 5-1 win at Loftus Road. Grimsby Town were now all that stood between the Hoops and a place in the last eight – and the Mariners were brushed aside with goals from Stainrod, Allen and Ernie Howe in a 3-1 win. Rangers received another home tie in the last eight and a tense encounter was settled by Allen's 88th minute strike, sending the Hoops into the FA Cup semi-final for the first time where they would face West Bromwich Albion at Highbury. Despite being the underdogs, Rangers fought valiantly with Bob Hazell superb at the back, nullifying the explosive Cyrille Regis. With the game evenly poised, Albion defender Ally Robertson attempted a clearance that struck Allen and ended up in the back of the West Brom net. The R's clung on valiantly to claim their place in the 1982 FA Cup final where they would face holders Tottenham. Again, the final was a tense affair with little in the way of entertaining football and ended 0-0 after normal time, but Glenn Hoddle's deflected drive put Spurs ahead on 109 minutes. All seemed lost for Venables' brave side until Hazell's nod on from a thrown-in was headed home by Terry Fenwick with just five minutes left, forcing a replay. With Allen absent from the replay, Spurs won the game with a sixth minute penalty through Hoddle, ending an incredible effort from Venables' side.

LEFT Simon Stainrod and John Gregory, having swapped shirts with Spurs players at the end of the match, 1982

Fenwick, Terry

(1980 – 87)

THOUGH TERRY FENWICK BEGAN his career as a full-back, he would spend the majority of his QPR career as a central defender and go on to win a record number of England caps while at Loftus Road. One of Terry Venables' first signings as Rangers boss, the Hoops paid £100,000 for the cultured defender in December 1980 and Fenwick went straight into the team and rarely left it from that moment on. Under Venables' expert guidance, Fenwick developed into a fine footballer and the move from full-back to centre-half during the 1981/82 season was arguably the making of him. He also won eight England Under-21 caps during his first few seasons with the R's. Fenwick scored the equalising goal in the 1982 FA Cup final against Spurs and became the club's resident penalty king notching 10 goals during the 1983/84 campaign, finishing second top scorer behind Simon Stainrod. In May 1984, he won his first full England cap against Wales and went on to win 19 caps while with QPR and also took part in the World Cup at Mexico in 1986. After almost exactly seven years with Rangers, Fenwick opted to move to Tottenham in a £550,000 deal.

Player stats:

Apps 307 + 1 sub

Goals 45

RIGHT Terry Fenwick keeps an eye on the ball

FAR RIGHT Les Ferdinand

Ferdinand, Les

(1986 – 95)

FEW REALISED THE SIGNIFICANCE of the 1987 signing of Les Ferdinand from non-league Hayes. QPR had invested just £15,000 in the 20-year-old striker's services and as nobody had really heard of him, if he disappeared into the ether, it was a gamble that hardly broke the bank so who cared? Indeed, for the first three years of his time at Loftus Road, Ferdinand failed to make a favourable impression of any kind at all, managing just two goals in the best part of three years – though they did both come in one game against Chelsea! He was loaned out to Brentford and Besiktas, helping the Turkish side – who sacrificed a sheep in his honour on his debut - to a league and cup double with 21 goals in 32 games. He returned to London a more confident player and when he was given his chance in the first team by Don Howe, he took it. He linked well with Roy Wegerle and a spell of seven goals in seven games during the latter half of the 1990/91 season helped Rangers to safety, making Ferdinand something of

Player stats:

Apps 163
Goals 80

a cult hero with the supporters. He was an explosive talent and it was clear he was something of a late bloomer, playing just half of the 1991/92 league matches (due to a broken cheekbone) but still scoring 10 valuable goals. Ferdinand always played with a trademark grin and his pace, power and ability soon caught the attention of several top clubs. By 1992/93, he'd made the No.9 jersey his own by scoring 24 goals in 42 appearances, earning him the nickname "Sir Les" by the adoring QPR fans, particularly as his exploits meant Rangers had finished as the top London side that year. Two more seasons of excellence, during which time he established himself in the England team and Ferdinand's departure became more a matter of when, rather than if. Eventually, Newcastle United manager Kevin Keegan offered £6m for one of the QPR's most popular players in recent years and the Hoops' board accepted the offer, much to the disappointment of the Rangers fans, many of whom cited the club's relegation a year later as a direct result of the sale.

Francis, Gerry

(1969 – 1979) & Manager
(1991 – 94 & 1998 – 2001)

ONE OF QPR'S FAVOURITE SONS, Gerry Francis' involvement with the club spanned more than three decades - as a player (during which time he became the first Rangers player to cap-tain England) - and then as manager.

A product of the R's successful youth policy, it was clear Francis was a gifted midfielder even in his mid-teens, with his vision, control and technique setting him apart from his peers – Francis was clearly destined for great things. He made his senior debut as a 17-year-old, coming on as substitute during a 2-1 defeat at Liverpool. He was handed a

LEFT Les Ferdinand in action, 1991

BELOW Gerry Francis delights his team's supporters with a goal

Player stats:	
Apps	347 + 7 sub
Goals	65

full league debut the following season, marking the occasion with a goal in a 3-1 victory over Portsmouth – one of a dozen starts that season as manager Les Allen eased his precocious talent into the side gently. The problem was, Francis was too good to leave out and when Gordon Jago took over as boss, he gave Francis the No.8 jersey and from then on, only injury kept him out of the team. With Rodney Marsh gone and Stan Bowles in, Francis became the main source of creativity in the side and struck up excellent understandings with both Bowles and Don Givens, as well as having an eye for goal himself. By the 1973/74 campaign, Francis was regarded as one of the best players in England and won five Under-23 caps that season.

He became a pivotal part of Dave Sexton's excellent mid-seventies Rangers team the following year and won his first full England cap against Czechoslovakia in 1974, becoming a regular for his country for the next two years and earning 12 caps – eight of which were as captain. When QPR finished runners-up to Liverpool in 1975/76, Francis was at his very peak, finishing second-top scorer with 12 goals as the R's agonisingly missed out on the title by a point. A back injury then robbed Rangers and England of a fantastic talent and he appeared in just 24 of the club's next 84 league matches, losing his place in the national team and never really re-discovering the kind of form that had made him an idol to the QPR fans.

There were fleeting glimpses of the Francis of old during the 1978/79 campaign but he moved across London to Crystal Palace in 1979 after the club accepted a bid of £450,000. Six months later, he was re-signed by the R's for a knock-down £150,000, reclaiming the No.8 jersey, but the magic had faded with the injury clearly still affecting him and he played his last match against Rotherham United before moving to Coventry as his career began to wind down, ending his career with Exeter City. He then moved into management, first with Exeter and then Bristol Rovers, where he turned a struggling Third Division side into a respected Division Two outfit. When the inevitable call came to manage QPR, he jumped at the chance to return to Loftus Road. In his second season he guided the club to their highest

Premiership finish – fifth – confirming the Hoops as London's top club for 1992/93. Successive mid-table finishes followed before Francis left to become Tottenham boss in November 1994. He wasn't quite finished at QPR, however, and returned as manager in 1998, helping keep the club clear of relegation for successive seasons before resigning as boss in February 2001. He recommended Ian Holloway, who'd played under Francis at both Bristol Rovers and QPR, as the new manager and became Director of Football for a brief period before returning to Bristol Rovers for a second spell in charge. The spark seemed to have gone for Francis, however, who quit the Pirates just six months later to concentrate on his businesses outside of football. He remains, however, a club legend and one of QPR's favourite sons.

LEFT Gerry Francis in his last match as manager during the game against Wimbledon

Francis, Trevor

(1988 – 90)

& Manager(1988 – 89)

RIGHT AND FAR
RIGHT Trevor Francis at
the top of his game

WHEN TREVOR FRANCIS JOINED the Super Hoops on a free transfer from Glasgow Rangers in 1988, it's fair to say he was well past his best as a player, but perhaps the QPR board had other ideas

for the former England international. Yet despite his advancing years, Francis still had enough in his locker to show some classy touches and could still win a game virtually single-handedly – as Aston Villa discovered to their cost after Francis fired a hat-trick against them in 1989. By that time, Francis had replaced the man who took him to Loftus Road – Jim Smith – in the role of player-

manager, but it was to be a difficult baptism in management for the 52-times capped striker. Francis guided QPR to a ninth-placed top-flight finish in his first campaign as player-boss, but the club were struggling near the bottom of the table during his second season and he was sacked as manager and replaced by his first team coach, Don Howe. During Francis' time in the hot-seat, he brought in experienced players such as Peter Reid and Nigel Spackman and signed Andy Sinton from Brentford for £300,000, but famously fined Martin Allen for missing a game due to the birth of his first child – something that didn't go down too well with the club's supporters, bearing in mind the Allen family history at QPR. His last act as manager was to arrange the signing of Ray Wilkins and he left Loftus Road in January 1990 on a free transfer to Sheffield Wednesday.

Furlong, Paul

(2000 & 2002 – 07)

RIGHT Paul Furlong tries to get to the ball before Paddy McCarthy of Leicester City

PAUL FURLONG ARGUABLY SPENT the best years of his career with QPR and gave excellent service during his five years at Loftus Road. Initially loaned in 2000 from Birmingham City, where his

career had stalled somewhat, Furlong played three times for the R's, scoring one goal in his three-game spell. When Ian Holloway became QPR boss in 2001, he brought Furlong back to the club on loan and after working with specialist forward coach Gary Penrice, Holloway told Furlong he believed he could get him back to somewhere near his best. The strapping forward scored twice in six appearances and Holloway negotiated a permanent deal for the player. By now aged 33, Holloway used Furlong in spells comparing him to a Rolls Royce that is taken out of the garage, driven occasionally before being polished and put back into storage! He scored a number of important goals for the R's, becoming a huge crowd favourite in the process, capped by his Player of the Year award in 2005. Furlong gave excellent service during his five years with the Hoops before moving to Luton Town in 2007. He dedicated his first goal for the Hatters to his friend Ray Jones, who had died just a few hours earlier.

Gallen, Kevin
(1992 – 2000 & 2001 – 07)

THOUGH KEVIN GALLEN WILL always hold a special place in QPR fans' hearts, he never really fulfilled the potential he showed as a teenager. Signed on as a schoolboy, Gallen was a phenomenon at youth team level where he scored an incredible 153 goals in 110 appearances for the R's, breaking the legendary Jimmy Greaves' goal-scoring record in youth football. Promotion to the first team saw the 19-year-old Gallen make his debut away to Manchester United for the 1994/95 curtain-raiser where he partnered Les Ferdinand. The pair quickly formed an intelligent partnership during that first season. Ferdinand's departure the following year saw the goals dry up for Gallen and in 1996/97 he sustained a

Player stats:

Apps	339 + 63 sub
Goals	97

LEFT Kevin Gallen scores under the challenge of Lee Naylor of Wolves

ABOVE Kevin Gallen leaves the field to a standing ovation

serious knee injury against Portsmouth and missed the rest of the season. A skilful forward, excellent at holding the ball and bringing others into play, Gallen's career with the Hoops was a rollercoaster affair that ebbed and flowed. Always popular with the fans, even through difficult periods, injuries and failure to gel with any strike partner in particular meant that he often found himself out in the cold as various managers brought in other forwards in an effort to spruce up the front line.

Gallen finally quit the R's in 2000, embarking on a 12-month stint in West Yorkshire, first with Huddersfield Town and then Barnsley, though sandwiched in between those two clubs he was back for pre-season training at QPR with a view to a permanent deal. His wages proved a stumbling block and he instead signed for Barnsley. The pull of Loftus Road, however, proved too strong and new manager Ian Holloway finally brought Gallen home in November 2001. He marked his return by scoring in a 4-0 win over Swindon Town. Gallen, a more rounded and mature player by that time enjoyed a much happier second spell at Loftus Road, earning the skipper's armband and becoming a talismanic figure among the supporters. Holloway's decision to give Gallen the added responsibility was inspired and he repaid his manager's faith in full, ironically following him to Plymouth Argyle on loan in 2007. Though offered a permanent deal at Home Park, he opted instead to sign for MK Dons, bringing a 14-year association with QPR to a close – for now! A terrific club servant, Gallen remains the last Rangers player to score in the Premier League and is the sixth highest goal-scorer in the club's history.

Gillard, Ian

(1968 – 1982)

ONLY TWO PLAYERS HAVE PLAYED more games for QPR than Ian Gillard, one of the club's greatest servants. The ever-dependable left-back, along with right-back Dave Clement would form a perfect balance for the R's defence for almost a decade with Gillard No.2 and Clement No.3 seemingly permanent names on the Hoops' team-sheet during the seventies. Gillard joined the club as a 16-year-old in 1966, making his senior debut during a 2-1 victory over Nottingham Forest in November 1968, but his opportunities were limited for the first few years under manager Les Allen, resulting in Gillard asking Allen's replacement, Gordon Jago, for a transfer. His request was turned down and he didn't pin down the position until midway through the 1973/74 campaign, impressing Jago and then Dave Sexton and rarely missing a game thereafter. He won international recognition with the England Under-23s before winning the first of three full caps in 1974. When full-back partner Dave Clement left in 1979, Gillard's Rangers career continued for another three years and he bowed out at the top, by making his final two appearances for the club in the 1982 FA Cup final and subsequent replay against Spurs before moving to Aldershot, just two months after his Wembley appearance.

BELOW Ian Gillard, 1976

Player stats:

Apps	479 + 5 sub
Goals	11

Givens, Don

(1972 – 78)

DON GIVENS PROVED TO BE A terrific buy for manager Gordon Jago. The Republic of Ireland international cost just £40,000 in July 1972 and went on to become one of the club's most prolific scorers over a six-year spell at Loftus Road. The former Manchester United junior actually played for his country twice before he played for United and the Limerick-born forward made just eight starts for the Reds before moving to Luton Town. Givens continued to represent Ireland during his two years at Kenilworth Road, averaging a goal every four games for the Hatters. An excellent, old fashioned-style striker, Givens added a new dimension to the R's attack, but Jago's masterstroke was to purchase Stan Bowles as his strike partner and the pair instantly struck up an understanding. The goals flowed and Givens found the net 26 times in his first campaign. His consistency played an integral part of arguably the best QPR team ever in the mid-seventies and while Bowles' flair and invention grabbed most of the headlines, Givens kept doing what he did best; scoring goals and he became Ireland's most-capped player during his time with the club. His final season was his least productive, managing just four strikes in 37 league games after which he joined Birmingham City for £150,000.

Player stats:

Apps	293 + 1 sub
Goals	101

RIGHT Don Givens playing against West Ham United

Goals, Goals, Goals!

QPR'S RECORD VICTORY came on December 3, 1960 when Tranmere Rovers were put to the sword during a Division Three clash at Loftus Road. Rangers won 9-2 to eclipse an 8-1 hammering of Bristol Rovers during a 1937 FA Cup tie. QPR came within one goal of setting a new record in 1983 with another 8-1 win, this time against Crewe Alexander in the League Cup – each victory remains a club record in each competition.

On the flip side, there are two 8-1 scorelines QPR fans don't want to be reminded of too often – a 1965 Division Three drubbing by Mansfield Town and a 1969 Division One thrashing by Manchester United – one of those losses is slightly easier to swallow than the other!

Rodney Marsh's fantastic 44-goal haul during the 1966/67 season is a record that has stood for more than 40 years and will prove difficult to beat, while legendary striker George Goddard is the club's leading career goal-scorer with 172.

ABOVE Rodney Marsh, who scored 44 goals in 53 games during the 1966/67 season

Goddard, George

(1926 – 33)

Player stats:

Apps   259
Goals 189

THE GREATEST GOAL-SCORER IN QPR's history, George Goddard was a goal machine that wrote his name into the club's record books with his incredible predatory instincts.

Goddard was signed from Redhill after word spread of his exploits at amateur level. He'd been working for a local bus company but when the R's offered him a professional contract in June 1926, the 23-year-old jumped at the chance to follow his dream. He made his debut against Brentford the following September, wearing the No.9 jersey and starting as he meant to go on with a goal during a 4-2 defeat, completed the season with 23 goals from 38 starts. For the 1927/28 season he found the net 26 times in 34 games before hitting his peak over the next two campaigns by scoring 38 and 39 meaning he had passed the 100 goals milestone in under three and a half seasons with the R's – a phenomenal achievement. Goddard's totals decreased each season

thereafter, managing 29, then 19 and finally 15 in his last campaign with the club. He made his final appearance against Northampton in September 1933 before moving to Brentford a couple of months later having failed to find the net in his last dozen games for the Hoops.

Gregory, Jim
Chairman 1965 – 1987

BORN IN 1928, JIM GREGORY WAS A boyhood Rangers fan who was born in Hammersmith and raised in Shepherds Bush. Forced into business by his father's involvement in the Second World War, Gregory ran the family fish stall from the age of 14 until his father returned, by which time his son had a taste for business, initially in second-hand cars. By the end of the 1950s, he'd built up a successful trade and was the proud owner of Gregory's Motordome in Hounslow. His sharp business acumen saw him venture into various ventures and he always seemed to make money on any deal he entered into. Sufficiently wealthy enough to impress the QPR board, he joined as a director towards the end of 1964 and seemed a natural choice to take over as chairman a few months later. A dynamic character with the club close to his heart, he began to use his wealth to raise the club's profile, developing Loftus Road and funding manager Alec Stock's team building, most notably with the £15,000 purchase of Rodney Marsh from Fulham in 1966. It was no coincidence that the R's

LEFT Chairman Jim Gregory, (l), congratulates Manager Jim Smith, 1986

achieved three successive promotions in Gregory's first three seasons as chairman, going from Division Three South to Division One as well as winning the League Cup in 1967. Gregory had accomplished his dream of seeing the R's in the top-flight much earlier than even he'd dared to dream and even though the team spent just one year in the top division before being relegated, Gregory was still at the helm when the club won promotion back to Division One four years later.

Gregory remained chairman until 1987, stepping down only on the advice of his doctor and selling the club to Marler Estates. Not long after leaving QPR, he became chairman at Portsmouth until the mid-1990s, until ill-health forced him to take things a little easier. Sadly, Jim Gregory passed away in 1998, though his influence on the club he loved will never be forgotten by Rangers fans.

Gregory, John

(1981 – 85)

& Manager (2006 – 07)

MIDFIELDER JOHN GREGORY had played for Northampton Town, Aston Villa and Brighton & Hove Albion by the time he joined the R's in 1981 and had clocked up more than 300 league games – all reflected by the hefty £300,000 price tag then-boss Terry Venables was willing to pay for his services. He began life at Loftus Road in the No.2 jersey, making his debut against Wrexham during a 3-1 win and was a key member of the 1982 FA Cup final squad, playing in both Wembley clashes with Spurs as well as scoring 11 goals during an impressive first season. His second campaign with QPR was even better as he ended the 1982/83 campaign as an ever-present in the league with 15 goals in the bank, all of which contributed to his first England cap in 1983 against Australia. He would add five more during his time with the Super Hoops and Gregory's easy-on-the-eye style and technique fitted perfectly into the Rangers ethos. He was a popular player both on and off the pitch. Gregory enjoyed another two productive seasons with the club before joining Derby County early into the 1985/86 campaign for £100,000 and later moved into management, most notably with Aston Villa. In 2006, almost 20 years since leaving Loftus Road, he returned to manage the R's – he had constantly been linked with the job for several years so it was no surprise when speculation became reality, replacing Gary Waddock. Some fans took a dim view of Gregory's friendship with chairman Gianni Paladini and viewed the appointment with suspicion. His tenure, however, was not a happy one and QPR won just 13 of the 48 games he presided over and he was sacked in October 2007 after a string of poor results.

Player stats:

Apps	182 + 2 sub
Goals	43

Grounds

IT'S INCREDIBLE QUEEN'S PARK Rangers weren't formed as Queen's Park Nomads considering the club's list of grounds they have called home at one point or another. An embryonic QPR played their first game at Welford's Fields and stayed there until the club moved to their first enclosed ground, renting Brondesbury from London Scottish for £20 per year. The fact rugby was also being played on the same pitch meant the partnership became untenable and new accommodation was sought at Home Farm. That too, was deemed unsuitable and a short stay at Kensal Green Rise was followed by a spell at the Gun Club Ground at Wormwood Scrubs, then Kilburn County Cricket Ground before spending two years at Kensal Rise Athletic Ground between 1899 and 1901. A brief stint at Latimer Road in Notting Hill followed before the club returned to Kensal Rise following objections from local residents in Notting Hill, but it wasn't long before they were asked to pay a huge rent increase forcing yet another move, this time to the Royal Agricultural Society showground. The Hoops enjoyed a three-year stay there before moving to a new area within the grounds known as the Horse Ring – at least the pitch was in stable condition, though hoofing the ball was frowned upon.

After a now familiar three-year stay, the R's found a home at the brand new 60,000 capacity Park Royal Stadium in 1907, owned by the Great Western Railway and enjoyed a decade at the ground before the war meant the pitch was turned into allotments as rations and food shortages gripped the nation. Eventually, in 1917 QPR took over the pitch abandoned by Shepherd's Bush FC at Ellerslie Road, re-erected the stand from the Park Royal Stadium, refurbished offices and dressing rooms beneath the stand and took the name of Loftus Road. At last the R's had somewhere that felt like their own and remained the sole tenants for 14 years, before the board felt the increasing attendances merited a grander stage

and so upped sticks and moved down the road to the spacious White City Stadium with its 60,000 capacity. After considering a sale of the land, it was decided to keep Loftus Road for the club's reserve fixtures – a move that proved to be a very wise decision. White City was rarely more than a third full and by the start of the 1933/34 campaign QPR were back at Loftus Road – and stayed there for 29 years before again believing White City's larger capacity would attract more fans. It didn't happen and just 10 months later, the club returned to Loftus Road – and they've been there ever since!

BELOW Loftus Road

Hat-trick Heroes

QPR HAVE HAD THEIR FAIR share of hat-trick heroes, but five in particular are head and shoulders above the rest. First off, a respective nod in the direction of Peter Turnbull, who became the first Rangers player to score three goals in one game when he helped the R's to a 5-0 win over West Hampstead in the FA Cup. Fred Bevan and J Smith managed four hat-tricks apiece before two of the greatest strikers the club has ever seen began to score goals for fun. George Goddard bagged an incredible 16 hat-tricks between 1927 and 1932. Tommy Cheetham managed seven from 1935 to 1939 and W Heathcoate took nine match balls home with him between 1943 and 1945. Brian Bedford came within two trebles of the club record by netting 14 hat-tricks between

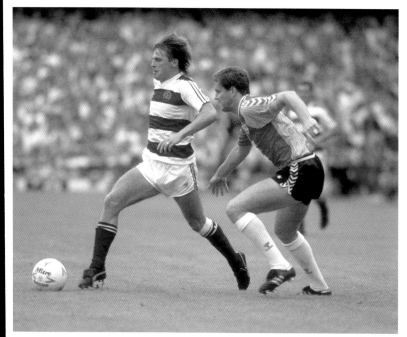

FAR LEFT Stan Bowles, scorer of four QPR hat-tricks

LEFT All four of Gary Bannister's trebles came when the R's were a top-flight side

1960 and 1964, but though impressive all these players were, none were at a level higher than Division Three. Six of Rodney Marsh's eight trebles came in either cup ties or Division Two matches, while Stan Bowles scored two in Europe, one in Division Two and one in Division One (though Don Givens was the first to notch a top-flight hat-trick for Rangers). Clive Allen scored two of his five hat-tricks in Division One, while Gary Bannister scored all four of his while QPR were a top-flight side – one of them in the UEFA Cup – making him one of the club's most successful strikers.

Hazell, Bob

(1979 – 83)

WHEN IT COMES TO STRAPPING, old-fashioned centre-halves, Jamaican-born Bob Hazell was right up there with the best of them. Built like a proverbial brick out-house, the no-nonsense Hazell signed for the R's in September 1979 for £240,000 from Wolves and made his debut in a 2-0 League Cup win over Bradford City, instantly making the No.5 shirt his own with a typically robust display. Hazell's ability was not purely based on physical strength, however, and he soon proved to be a valuable asset with his intelligent use of the ball. Injury kept him out of much of his second campaign with the club, but he was back to carve his name into Hoops folklore during the 1981/82 season. With the R's facing West Brom in the FA Cup semi-final at Highbury, Hazell was given the task of marking the powerful and prolific Cyrille Regis out of the game – a seemingly impossible task at a time he was the most feared forward in the country – yet Hazell did it with the performance of his life. The R's won 1-0 and Hazell's epic perform-ance meant a first FA Cup final for the club and big Bob played in both games against Spurs. The following season he helped Rangers back to the top-flight, playing 39 league games during the 1982/83 campaign before moving to Leicester City in September 1983 for £100,000

Player stats:

Apps   117 + 7 sub
Goals   9

RIGHT Bob Hazell, 1981

Hollins, John

(1975 – 79)

DESPITE RESERVATIONS AMONG some QPR fans about the signing of John Hollins – perhaps due to the 12 years he spent with Chelsea prior to joining – the £80,000 the R's paid the Blues for the services of the versatile Hollins, ultimately proved money well spent by manager Dave Sexton. Hollins was a well-respected figure in football and was adept at full-back or as a defensive midfielder and he added a touch of steel to Rangers, evident as Sexton's superb side began their quest for the previously unthinkable – the First Division league title. Hollins gave his usual accomplished performance on his debut against Liverpool as the R's posted a warning to the rest of the division with a 2-0 victory at Loftus Road and though Liverpool eventually clinched the title, they finished only a single point ahead of QPR. Hollins continued to give good value by clocking up 40 appearances in his second season, 39 in his third and 41 in what proved to be his final season with the club. He left for Arsenal aged 33 and the Gunners paid just £5,000 less than QPR had originally spent making Hollins one of the club's best pound-for-pound buys of the modern era.

Player stats:

Apps	177 + 6 sub
Goals	7

ABOVE John Hollins

Holloway, Ian

(1991 – 96)
& Manager (2001 – 06)

GERRY FRANCIS WAS BRISTOL Rovers' boss when he spotted Ian Holloway playing for Brentford. Francis had known Holloway from his days as an effervescent midfielder with Bristol Rovers a few years earlier and was surprised to see that his career had gone off the rails. He told "Ollie" that he could get him playing again and that he should return to Bristol Rovers and play in his team. Ollie accepted and was soon back to his best, inspiring the Pirates for the next four years with his infectious enthusiasm. When Francis left Twerton Park to become QPR manager in 1991, he soon returned for Holloway, paying Rovers £230,000 for the 28-year-old. An honest, hard-working pro, Holloway made 46 appearances for the R's in his first season and for the next four years Holloway never gave anything less than his all every time he played. When his hometown club Bristol Rovers offered him the role of player-manager in 1996, he left Loftus Road and began his management career, guiding Rovers through a difficult period and earning a place in the play-offs in his second season, though Northampton progressed to the final at Rovers' expense. Though his time with Rovers looked unspectacular on paper, in actual fact he'd done a wonderful job keeping the club afloat, balancing the books and still managing to get his team to play attractive football. When Gerry Francis resigned as manager of QPR in February 2001, he recommended Holloway as his replacement. Ollie was given the impossible task of saving the Hoops with just three months of the season to go, but it proved too great a task and Rangers slipped to the third tier of English football for the first time in 34 years. It gave Ollie the chance to clear out a lot of dead wood and bring through some of the club's promising youngsters. His first full season saw QPR consolidate their place as the big fish in a small pond, but it wasn't until the 2002/03 campaign that the R's showed they were ready to return to Division One football as they made it to the play-off final. Playing Cardiff City at the Millennium Stadium, the Hoops were the better team for long periods but were stung by a goal four minutes from the end of extra time. Ollie told his players to remember the pain they were feeling in the dressing room after that game and use it the following season, which they duly did as Rangers won promotion in 2003/04.

Player stats:

Apps   151 +
              20 sub
Goals   5

LEFT Ian Holloway, Manager, 2001

The club were in dire finicial straits throughout Ollie's time as manager and he proved a hugely popular figure with the supporters who admired his honesty and openness. He became famous for his off-the-wall after-match quotes and became a popular figure throughout football during his time with QPR. He left the club during the 2005/06 season and was replaced by Gary Waddock. An excellent servant both on and off the pitch, Ollie went on to become manager of Plymouth Argyle and later moved to Leicester City.

Ingham, Tony
(1950 – 63)

Player stats:

Apps 548
Goals 3

BELOW Tony Ingham, middle row, second from right

NOBODY HAS REPRESENTED Queen's Park Rangers more times than Tony Ingham did. The Yorkshire-born left-back enjoyed a 13-year stint with the R's and for almost a decade, was an ever-present in the team. Ingham was born in Harrogate and was playing football locally when he was spotted by Leeds United. The Lilywhites took the raw youngster on, giving him a contract on April 1, 1947 but he only made three appearances for Leeds – one each season he was with the club – before QPR took him on in June 1950 for the princely sum of £5,000. He made his debut for Rangers during a 2-1 defeat to Doncaster in November 1950, making 23 starts during his first season at Loftus Road. He added another 18 appearances before finally nailing the left-back spot down in 1952/53 with 46 starts and a truly rare goal – his first for the club – in a 4-2 loss at Crystal Palace. Ingham was 28 by the start of the 1953/54 campaign and was clearly a late bloomer – he became an integral member of the team during the mid-fifties and from February 1955 to September 1961, he didn't miss a single game – an incredible run of 250 consecutive league starts! He was 38 by the time he played his last game for the club during a 3-1 defeat at home to Coventry – his 548th start for the R's – a record that will take some beating.

Jago, Gordon
(Manager 1971 – 74)

GORDON JAGO WAS THRUST INTO English club management for the first time in 1971 following Les Allen's decision to quit QPR. Jago, a former Charlton Athletic centre-half had spent several years in the USA, eventually managing the US national side in 1969. It was to be a brief appointment, however, with Jago leaving his post after losing the two games he presided over. He returned to the UK, becoming Allen's assistant at Loftus Road before eventually moving into the hot-seat in January 1971. He guided the R's to a mid-table finish in Division Two and during his first full campaign in charge, Rangers finished fourth in the league, missing promotion by a single victory. By that time, Jago had sold Rodney Marsh to Manchester City and he bolstered his squad by signing the mercurial talents of Stan Bowles and Don Givens for the 1972/73 season and the pair shared 40 goals as the R's won promotion back to the top-flight. Dave Thomas and Frank McLintock proved Jago had an excellent eye in the transfer market and Rangers finished an impressive eighth in his first season in the First Division. However, he couldn't take the club any further and after a disastrous start to the 1974/75 season, Jago left for Millwall and was replaced by Dave Sexton.

ABOVE Gordon Jago

James, Leighton

(1977 – 78)

RIGHT Leighton James

A DASHING LEFT-WINGER, SHOULder length hair and a crowd pleaser to boot – surely the 24-year-old Leighton James was born to play for QPR? Everything seemed right when the exciting James signed for the R's in exchange for Don Masson, but somehow, things didn't quite work out as planned. James was already an established Wales international by the time he arrived at Loftus Road in October 1977 and his record at club level for Burnley and Derby County of 60 goals in under 250 games, suggested the 24-year-old would be a huge asset to Frank Sibley's side. Yet QPR were on the wane as the recently departed Dave Sexton's team began to break up and James seemed to struggle to adapt to London life. He made his debut during a 2-1 win over West Brom and missed just three games for the club during the remainder of the season. He was still at QPR for the start of the 1978/79 season, but when Sibley was replaced by Steve Burtenshaw, the end was nigh for James. When a bid of £165,000 came in from his old club

Burnley, the deal seemed acceptable to all parties and after playing his final match for the Hoops against the club he made his debut against – West Brom – James returned north to Turf Moor leaving Rangers fans to wonder about what might have been.

Jones, Ray

(2005 – 07)

ONE OF THE SADDEST ENTRIES IN this book has to be the tragic story of Ray Jones, a hugely popular Rangers player with enormous potential. Jones joined the R's youth team after being released by Colchester United in 2005 and the teenage striker soon impressed enough to be handed a first team debut against Watford towards the end of the 2005/06 season. By the start of the following campaign, Jones was regularly in or around the starting line-up and won an England Under-19 cap against Holland as his star continued to rise. His performances had a host of top clubs casting their eye over him and it seemed only a matter of time before the cash-strapped R's would be forced to sell the youngster. However, Jones pledged his future with QPR and signed a lengthy new deal at the start of 2007 after settling well at Loftus Road,

Player stats:	
Apps	18 + 19 sub
Goals	6

LEFT Shabazz Baidoo is congratulated by team mate Ray Jones

increasing his popularity further still among the supporters and management. He had all the attributes needed to become a top player and was brimming with confidence – perhaps he was even destined for the coveted No.10 jersey one day. Then, on the eve of 2007/08 season, Jones and two friends, Idris Olasupo and Jess Basilva, were killed in a horrific car accident in London. Jones was just three days short of his 19th birthday and his death robbed football of a glittering talent.

Rangers postponed their match with Burnley the next day as the club and fans came to terms with the shocking news. For the first home game of the campaign just a week later, the R's players all wore the name of Ray Jones on their back and the club retired his No.31 jersey permanently. A fantastic talent who Rangers fans believe would have been a huge star for club and country in future years, Jones was a genuinely nice kid and somebody Queen's Park Rangers FC will never forget.

RIGHT Floral tributes to Ray Jones left outside the stadium

Kit

ABOVE The Hoops in 2007

ONE OF THE MOST distinctive football kits in England – or anywhere for that matter – QPR's famous blue and white hoops are one of the main reasons the R's are such a unique football club. The club colours positively demand attractive football be played by the fortunate few to wear them and if the club ever decided to abandon them, there would be a mutiny in the Loft! For a time, Rangers played in green and white hoops – the colours of Celtic – and wore the strip from 1892 until 1927. However, the R's endured a torrid few years and twice had to fight for re-election after finishing bottom of Division 3 South in 1924 and 1926. The club decided to change the green hoops for blue ones, more in hope of a change of fortune than anything else – and it seemed to work! Rangers finished in the top half of the league for four successive seasons in the new kit, representing their most consistent spell since joining the league in 1920. After winning promotion to Division Two in 1948, the club appealed to the supporters to donate coupons in order to replace the tattered strip

KIT

BELOW Goalies' attire in the late 1940s

representative sides had used throughout the war years. The new kit was a sort of blue version of Arsenal's shirts and lasted one season before the popular blue and white hoops were restored. Superstitious to the last, when the R's were relegated four years later, they adopted plain white shirts with blue shorts for the next seven years. Sanity prevailed in 1960, the hoops were once again restored and QPR have worn those colours ever since.

Leach, Mick
(1964 – 78)

ABOVE Mick Leach

EVERY CLUB NEEDS AT LEAST ONE Mr Reliable in their squad – a 100 per cent honest pro who goes about his business quietly and efficiently over a sustained period of time. QPR's Mr Reliable was Mick Leach, an old fashioned centre-forward who joined the club as a youth player in 1964 and scored on his league debut against Colchester a year later, though he had to bide his time and wait for a decent run in the first team. It wasn't until the 1968/69 season that Leach was finally given the opportunity he'd been waiting for, playing 30 league games for the R's and repeating the feat the following season, cementing his place in the side. There was nothing fancy about his style of play and compared to the mercurial talents of Rodney Marsh and later Stan Bowles, he was positively ordinary – but Leach played with his heart on his sleeve and complemented his more gifted partners to great effect. As time went on, he was used less often, but whenever he was asked to do a job, he'd do it, even if it meant playing out of position or to the benefit of others and he scored a number of important goals for the club during his career. After clocking up 360 appearances for the Hoops, he made his final bow for the club during an FA Cup tie with Wealdstone in 1978 before flying out to try his luck in the NASL. Tragically, he died in 1992 from cancer, aged 45.

Player stats:

Apps	337 + 24 sub
Goals	70

RIGHT Loftus Road
bathed in sunshine

Loftus Road

SITUATED IN SHEPHERDS BUSH, London W12 with a capacity of 19,148, Loftus Road is one of the most famous football stadiums in England. Originally the home of Shepherds Bush FC, QPR took residence of the site in 1917 after playing their home matches at numerous venues around the capital and the ground was developed slowly over a period of time, thanks in no small measure to former chairman Jim Gregory, a lifelong Rangers fan who pumped chunks of his own personal fortune into making Loftus Road a home to be proud of. One of the tightest arenas in English football, Loftus Road was once the scourge of many a top side after a plastic pitch was laid in 1981 – an unpopular move, though perfectly legal, QPR soon mastered the surface to great effect. However, the harshness of the surface caused a number of injuries and burns over the years, and it was ripped up in 1988 and replaced with grass.

The highest attendance at the ground was in April 1974, when 35,353 watched QPR go down 1-0 to Leeds United.

Following the Taylor Report, Loftus Road became an all-seater stadium in time for the 1994/95 campaign, substantially reducing the capacity in the process.

The four stands are the Ellerslie Road Stand, South Africa Road Stand, the School End and the most famous of all, the Loftus Road End, known to one and all as "The Loft". It is home to the club's more vocal supporters and is the club's version of The Kop. The R's have shared the ground in the past – with London Wasps from 1996-2002 and Fulham from 2002 to 2004, who paid rent while Craven Cottage was redeveloped. It is believed there are no plans to expand the ground until the team can regularly fill the stadium to its current capacity.

Marsh, Rodney
(1966 – 72)

RIGHT Rodney Marsh
in action, 1970

DURING THE SEVENTIES THERE was Stan Bowles and Gerry Francis and later on there was Les Ferdinand – but first came Rodney Marsh – perhaps the club's most popular player ever. If ever a man was born to play for QPR, it was the magical Marsh who left an imprint on the club that is still evident today. That the club is associated with style, panache and an almost arrogant swagger on the pitch is almost entirely down to Marsh, one of the most gifted forwards this country has produced. He had everything – skill, flair and an abundance of natural ability – and to think he cost the club just £15,000 from Fulham. An inspired Alec Stock purchase, Marsh was the first player to make the No.10 shirt special, and

dozens of players have tried to live up to the association of individual brilliance with the jersey ever since. Having arrived at Loftus Road in March 1966, the 21-year-old made his league debut for the R's in the inauspicious surrounds of London Road during a 1-1 draw with Peterborough United. Yet his influence began to take hold just a game later, as he scored twice in a 6-1 win over Millwall, a side well on their way to promotion by that time. He then starred in successive 4-1 wins over Workington Town and Bristol Rovers meaning the Hoops had scored 15 goals in four games since his arrival. Marsh ended the campaign with eight goals from 16 starts, but of course, he was just at the beginning of a fantastic journey. His

greatest period came during his first full season with the club in 1966/67 – the unforgettable "double" season as QPR finally rocketed in the nation's consciousness with a quite breathtaking campaign in which Marsh was, quite simply, brilliant. The R's would score 103 goals in the league on their way to the Division 3 title and Marsh scored 30 of them. He scored another three in the FA Cup and added a phenomenal 11 in nine games as Rangers became the first third tier side to win the League Cup with a 3-2 win over West Brom – Marsh's superb individual goal forcing extra time while Wembley rocked to the chant of "Rod-nee! Rod-nee! Rod-nee!" His total of 44 goals in one season has never been bettered.

He was no less effective as the club pressed for successive promotions and he scored 14 goals in 25 starts during an injury-hit campaign that still saw the R's move into the top division for the first time ever. Was the success down to the "Marsh factor"? If it was, it was no coincidence that when his influence began to wane slightly, the team's fortunes also went into decline. Alec Stock's shock resignation prior to the 1968/69 season certainly had a negative effect on the

side and Rangers finished bottom of the league in their inaugural season at the top and Marsh scored just four times in 22 games. He scored 21 in 39 appearances the following season and 23 in 42 starts during the 1970/71 season as the Hoops began to look a very good side once again. Marsh finally won his first full England cap in November 1971, raising his profile yet higher and though the club had resisted numerous offers for their star forward's services over the years, when Manchester City offered £200,000 for him in March 1972, it was too big an offer to refuse. The mercurial star headed north leaving QPR to chase promotion without their talismanic No.10. Ironically, the R's didn't lose any of their remaining 12 games that season, conceding just two goals along the way to just missing out on promotion. As for Rodney, his individuality was cited as the reason Manchester City failed to win the Division One title they'd seemed destined to win with his maverick style seeming to disrupt the flow of what had been a finely-tuned machine. Of course, the City fans soon fell under his spell, but his true love will always be QPR and on quiet days, when the stadium is empty, you can still hear a distant chant of "Rod-nee!" faintly echo around Loftus Road…

Masson, Don

(1974 – 77)

DON MASSON WAS A TOUGH-AS-old-boots midfielder who arrived at Loftus Road approaching his 29th birthday. His unspectacular career had begun with Middlesbrough before transferring to Notts County and though he'd failed to win recognition with his home nation Scotland, manager Dave Sexton saw him as the ideal addition to his team. Masson was an unusual mix of hardened pro and creative midfielder and he initially took the No.4 jersey after making his debut in a 1-0 win over Sheffield United. While Masson had enjoyed a steady career, it hadn't reached the heights it perhaps should have, but at Loftus Road, he excelled and was the missing piece of Sexton's jigsaw – a velvet glove covering an iron fist. Masson was an ever-present during the 1975/76 season that saw Rangers miss out on the title to Liverpool by a point and he added six goals during a terrific campaign at the end of which he was rewarded with the first of 17 caps for Scotland, making his debut shortly before his 30th birthday.

Player stats:

Apps 144
Goals 24

Wearing the No.9 shirt, Masson finished second top-scorer with eight goals in his third season with the R's before moving to Derby County in October 1977 in a straight swap with Leighton James.

ABOVE Don Masson (r) tackling Alan Curbishley of West Ham, 1977

McDonald, Alan

(1981 – 97)

RIGHT Alan McDonald challenges Mark Hughes of Manchester United

ONE OF THE CLUB'S MOST LOYAL servants, Alan McDonald became a permanent fixture in the QPR side for the best part of two decades after progressing through the club's youth ranks. The teenage centre-half initially found it difficult to break into the first team at Loftus Road so was happy to accept a loan deal with Charlton Athletic towards the end of the 1982/83 season. He made nine starts for the Addicks before returning back to the R's a more experienced and determined player, so when Bob Hazell left for Leicester City in September 1983, it was McDonald who staked a claim for the vacant No.5 shirt. He made an impressive debut during a 4-0 win away at Wolves and two weeks later he'd scored his first senior goal as the R's thrashed Crewe 8-1 at Loftus Road. Despite the promising start, he then drifted out of the team, filling in for injured or suspended players for the next 18 months. Jim Smith was then installed as the new QPR boss for the start of the

1985 season and as often happens many of the fringe first team players began with a clean slate. For McDonald, it meant a permanent starting place as Smith utilised the Northern Irish defender at both centre-half and full-back during his first campaign in charge and McDonald missed just one of the R's 52 matches during the 1985/86 season. From there on, McDonald was one of the first names on the team-sheet, winning his first cap for Northern Ireland in 1986 and becoming the bedrock of the defence. He was rewarded with a testimonial in 1989, but was a long way from finished at QPR. In fact, he was about halfway through his career, taking on the No.6 jersey in the 1990s and clocking up close to 500 appearances before joining Swindon Town on a free transfer in 1997, retiring as a player a year later.

Uncompromising in the tackle, McDonald was a great leader on the pitch and with 16 years service, man and boy, he was QPR through and through. With 52 appearances for his country – many as captain – he remains the most-capped player in the club's history and he returned to Loftus Road, briefly, as Gary Waddock's assistant in 2006 but left shortly after John Gregory's arrival.

McLintock, Frank

(1973 – 77)

Player stats:

Apps   162+
        1 sub
Goals   6

FRANK MCLINTOCK BEGAN LIFE as wing-half with Leicester City and enjoyed seven years at Filbert Street before transferring to Arsenal in 1964. During his time at Highbury, McLintock moved from midfield to central defence and became an integral part of a successful Gunners team during the late sixties and early seventies. He was made captain in 1967 and led the team twice at Wembley in successive League Cup finals in 1968 and 1969, but each time he ended up with a runners-up medal and feeling totally deflated, he asked for a transfer. Persuaded to stay by manager Bertie Mee, McLintock went on to skipper the side to a league and FA Cup double in 1971. Despite being 34, Dave Sexton was convinced the tough Scot could help lead his side to unscaled heights and he signed McLintock on in June 1974 for a fee of £30,000. McLintock was a winner and he made the No.5 shirt his own averaging more than 30 appearances a season during his time at Loftus Road. McLintock was the defensive rock that enabled Sexton's attractive side to play with freedom and he represented excellent value for his influence and the appearances he made while a Rangers player. He retired after the 1976/77 campaign having made more than 700 career appearances and later moved into management.

Mittal, Lakshmi

WHEN INDIAN STEEL MAGNATE Lakshmi Mittal was told by his old friend Bernie Ecclestone that he should join him and Flavio Briatore by investing in Queens Park Rangers FC, he decided to do exactly that, pushing Rangers into the super wealthy league when it came to owner/investors. For a club that went into administration under Ian Holloway's reign as manager and once had two supporters buy them a player, Mittal's decision to purchase a 20 per cent holding in the club, was a manna from heaven. Born in Sadulpur, India, Mittal owns 44 per cent of ArcelorMittal, the world's largest steel company. He began his career by working in the family steel business, but in 1994 he took over the company's international operations and later became the president of the board of directors. His personal fortune is estimated to be £26billion, making him – allegedly – the fifth richest man in the world. He once spent £30m on his daughter's wedding and will be represented on the board by his son-in-law Amit Bhatia. What this all means for the club in terms of spending power will become clearer as time goes by, but at least Rangers fans can claim to be – at least on paper – the wealthiest club in West London – make that England – and Europe…probably the world.

FAR LEFT
Dave Thomas and Dave Clements flank a jubilant Frank McLintock

BELOW Lakshmi Mittal

Morgan Twins

Morgan, Roger
(1964 – 69)

Morgan, Ian
(1964 – 73)

Player stats:

Apps   206
Goals   44

RIGHT Ian Morgan

THE MORGAN TWINS, ROGER AND Ian, became an integral part of QPR during the 1960s and together clocked up nearly 400 appearances for the club. Roger was the better of the two brothers who must have confused any number of full-backs with Roger on one wing and Ian on the other – only their shirt numbers (unless they swapped them at half-time) gave a clue as to who was who. Both signed on as apprentices in September 1964 and it was Ian who broke into the senior team first, making his debut aged 17 during a 2-1 win against Hull City and he set up one of the goals. Roger made his debut in the next match against Gillingham – the first time the twins had played for QPR at the same time. Both were fast and skilful and popular with the fans, but

Roger became something of a crowd idol during his time at Loftus Road. He became a permanent fixture in the first team, while Ian had to fight for a place and his appearances just about edged into double figures for a number of years. Both were named in the team for the 1967 League Cup final against West Brom, but while Roger started and scored the goal that got the R's back into the game at 2-1, Ian was an unused substitute. The pair's most productive season as a pair came during Rangers' superb 1967/68 Division Two campaign, with Ian an ever-present playing in all 46 games the club took part in that season, enjoying his best haul of goals – 10. The following campaign would be Roger's last at Loftus Road after the Hoops accepted a club record fee of £110,000 from Tottenham for his services in February 1969. It was heart-breaking news for the Rangers' supporters,

particularly as his first game for Spurs was against QPR! Ian Morgan remained with Rangers but his first team opportunities became fewer and fewer as the seasons passed and eventually, in October 1973, he joined Watford for £10,000.

BELOW Roger Morgan

Player stats:

Apps	175 + 14 sub
Goals	28

New Year's Day

THE FIRST DAY of 1992 will always hold a special place in the hearts of QPR fans thanks to one man; Lambeth-born Dennis Bailey, a man that Rangers supporters – and Manchester United fans – will not forget in a hurry. On New Year's Day 1992, the Hoops travelled to Old Trafford, a place they had never previously won, and with only five wins in the league going into January, the outlook seemed bleak for Gerry Francis' men. Dennis Bailey, however, had other ideas… Andy Sinton put Rangers one up before Bailey raced through to hit a shot powerfully enough to make it 2-0 after five minutes. His second of the game came after the break when he raced to the edge of the box and chipped the ball over Schmeichel to make it 3-0 and his hat-trick came when Sinton's shot hit the post and fell at Bailey's feet two yards out to give him the simplest of tap-ins to complete a memorable 4-1 victory. It was undoubtedly the greatest day of Bailey's career. He played just four more games before sustaining an injury that kept him out until the final game of the season. Seventeen years on, he remains that last Englishman to score a hat-trick at Old Trafford. Hallelujah!

Ouch!

IN 1981, IT'S SAFE TO SAY THAT Loftus Road became the least looked forward to venue for opposing teams and their players after the Hoops decided to dig up their grass pitch and replace it with Astroturf - the first English club to do so. It was a bold but ultimately ill-fated decision that was condemned by the football community, even though several more English clubs soon followed suit and also laid what became commonly known as "plastic pitches". Ironically, one of them, Luton Town, were the first team to play on the new Loftus Road surface and the Hatters won 2-1 – no doubt encouraging them to acquire one themselves, which they duly did, becoming the second club to have one!

However, though the R's soon became used to plastic and learned how

ABOVE The first League fixture on Astroturf

FAR LEFT Dennis Bailey

to get the most from the surface, it became a common sight to see players wearing black tights and sustaining unusual injuries – most akin to carpet burns! Players recovering from knee injuries despised the surface, the bounce was never true and sprinkling sand across the pitch didn't help matters, either. It wasn't until 1988 that Loftus Road's playing surface returned to grass with the painful plastic surface ripped up and consigned to history for good – thank God!

Parker, Paul
(1987 – 91)

PAUL PARKER LOOKED AN OUT-standing prospect when he broke into Fulham's first team in 1982 and the speedy full-back was constantly watched by a host of top sides, though nobody seemed willing to take a gamble on the young Londoner. He remained at Craven Cottage for five seasons, clocking up more than 150 appearances for the club and earning eight England Under-21 caps before QPR boss Jim Smith offered £200,000 for the player, which the cash-strapped Cottagers surprisingly accepted. Parker soon settled into the Rangers team in central defence and his steady, reliable presence helped the R's to a fifth-placed finish in the old Division One. Parker appeared in all 48 games the club played that season and added another 47 starts to his total during the 1988/89 campaign. In 1989, he also won the first of 19 full England caps, making his debut against Albania as a right-back and later winning a place in the 1990 World Cup squad in which he helped England to the semi-final. He missed much of his fourth and final season with the R's through injury and prior to the 1991/92 campaign, he joined Manchester United for a club record of £2m.

Parkes, Phil

(1970 – 79)

REG ALLEN, DAVID SEAMAN, CHRIS Woods, Peter Springett or Phil Parkes – the debate as to who is QPR's best goalkeeper of all time will continue to rage for as long as the club exists, but for those who grew up in or around the 1970s, it is Parkes all the way. Parkes was unfortunate to have been around when there were so many other top English keepers and had it not been for Peter Shilton, Ray Clemence and Joe Corrigan, Parkes would surely have been a regular England player for the best part of a decade. It was Les Allen who brought the 6' 3" shot-stopper to Loftus Road, paying Walsall just £15,000 for his services in June 1970. He made his debut in a 3-1 home defeat to Leicester City – his first of 109 consecutive appearances for the R's. In fact, he missed just two games during his first six seasons at Loftus Road – an incredible record during which time he became Mr Dependable, helping the club to previously unchartered heights in the topflight in the mid-seventies. Though he won seven England Under-23 caps, his only full cap came against Portugal in April 1974 and even then he kept a clean sheet. Parkes had made more than 406 starts for Rangers before he transferred to West Ham in February 1979. The £565,000 fee the club received was a world record amount for a keeper at the time and he enjoyed a successful spell with the Hammers, winning the FA Cup in his first full season at Upton Park.

FAR LEFT AND BELOW Phil Parkes, one of the greatest QPR 'keepers of modern times

Player stats:

Apps   406

Peacock, Darren

(1990 – 94)

DESPITE HAVING A HAIR STYLE similar to singer Michael Bolton,

Bristol-born Darren Peacock became a firm favourite with the QPR fans following his December 1990 move from Hereford United. Then aged 22, the giant centre-back cost £200,000 and made his debut against Derby County during a 1-1 draw, taking the No.5 shirt, which he would wear throughout his time with the club. He was part of the Rangers side that beat Liverpool 3-1 at Anfield in 1991 and also in the team that beat Manchester United 4-1 at Old Trafford on New Year's Day 1992 – two epic milestones in the club's history and he was consistent and dependable in defence. His form had not gone un-noticed however and he was constantly being watched by other clubs so it came as no surprise when Kevin Keegan's Newcastle United coughed up £2.7m for him in 1994. A good club servant, he was offered the chance to return to Loftus Road after struggling with form and injuries with his next club, Blackburn Rovers, but is believed to have turned down the chance to return to West London and retired from football in 2000, aged 32, after damaging vertebrae in his neck while on loan with Wolves. He currently works as a defensive coach at Newcastle.

Player stats:

Apps	141 + 3 sub
Goals	7

Peacock, Gavin

(1984 – 87 & 1996 – 2002)

GAVIN PEACOCK HAD TO LEAVE QPR to really kick-start his career having been with the club as a junior. He made his debut at home to Sheffield Wednesday in November 1986 and scored his only goal during his first spell

Player stats:

Apps   207 + 19 sub
Goals   42

RIGHT Gavin Peacock in action, 2000

with Rangers in the return match against the Owls later that season in a 7-1 defeat! He made a total of 17 appearances for the R's before being initially loaned to Gillingham and then signed permanently in 1987 for a £40,000 fee. An attacking midfielder by trade, he remained with the Gills for two years before being snapped up by Harry Redknapp at Bournemouth. Peacock stayed with the Cherries for a season before winning his biggest move to date with a £150,000 transfer to Newcastle United. After three years he moved to Chelsea for £1.25m, enjoying three successful years at Stamford Bridge before returning to Loftus Road in 1996 on loan, then signing permanently shortly after in a £800,000 deal. By then 29, Peacock became the Hoops' skipper and made more than 200 appearances over a six-year period, briefly spending time with Charlton on loan in 2001, before retiring from the game. A Christian, he once held bible groups for younger players at QPR and moved into television punditry with the BBC before quitting in 2008 to take a three-year Masters course in Divinity with the intention of possibly becoming a vicar, minister or pastor in the future.

Prince, Kiyan

KIYAN PRINCE WAS A YOUNG with immense promise who was murdered outside the gates of his school, The London Academy in Edgware, in May 2006. Kiyan had been with QPR since 2004 and was considered to have a very bright future in the game. Described as an "outstanding and upstanding boy", Kiyan intervened when he saw another boy being bullied

and was fatally stabbed – he was just 15-years-old. His attacker was quickly apprehended and arrested while Kiyan's family and the football club came to terms with his shocking death. Rangers revealed that they were planning to offer Kiyan, who had finished top scorer for the QPR Under-16 side for 2005/06, a professional contract after impressing the club's youth coaches. Rangers' manager at the time, Gary Waddock, said, "The whole club is mourning the loss of one of our own. We are all devastated. Kiyan was certainly one for the future, a talented lad who wanted to forge a career in football." Head of youth for the club, Joe Gallen, added, "He was a great lad, a terrific prospect and it's a huge setback for everyone that knew him."

Adored by family and friends, Rangers officials and fans wanted to ensure the memory of Kiyan lived on and after considering various ways to commemorate the youngster, the club's Goal of the Season award was re-named the Kiyan Prince Goal of the Season. Players and supporters observed a minute's silence before QPR's game against Southend at Loftus Road in August 2006.

LEFT A message of condolence is left in memory of Kiyan Prince outside QPR's ground

QPR

THE ORIGINS OF QUEEN'S PARK Rangers Football Club go back to 1882, with the founding of two youth clubs on a newly-built residential estate in West London. Christchurch Rangers were formed by George Wodehouse senior and St Jude's Institute were initiated by Jack McDonald and Fred Weller as an outlet for the boys of Droop Street Board School, they also received excellent support from Reverend Gordon Young. None of those gentlemen could ever have imagined that the football teams they helped bring into existence would one day become one of the top clubs in the country and 120 years later would still be flourishing – let alone be valued as one of the richest clubs in the world! The idea of merging the two teams together came in 1886, after

Christchurch and St Jude's had played each other and just a couple of weeks later, it was agreed that two should become one. At a meeting arranged to plan the way forward for the new club, it was suggested by a man called E D Robertson that, as the clubs had both been based in the Queen's Park district of London, they should be called Queen's Park Rangers – the name seemed perfect and was duly voted in and registered with the relevant authorities. After competing in various competitions and local amateur leagues, QPR became a professional club in 1899, taking their place in the Southern League Division One.

Records

Attendance:
35,353 v Leeds United, Division One, 27/4/73

Victory: 9-2 v Tranmere Rovers, Division Three, 3/12/60

8-1 v Bristol Rovers, FA Cup, 27/11/37

8-1 v Crewe Alexandra, League Cup, 3/10/83

Defeat: 1-8 v Mansfield Town, Division Three, 15/3/65

1-8 v Manchester United, Division One, 19/3/69

Most goals in one season:
44 – Rodney Marsh 1966/67

Most career goals:
189 George Goddard

Most capped player:
52 caps Alan McDonald – Northern Ireland

Record transfer received:
£6m Les Ferdinand – to Newcastle United 1995

Youngest player to represent QPR:
Frank Sibley, 15 yrs, 275 days old

Oldest player to represent QPR:
Ray Wilkins, 39 yrs, 352 days old

BELOW A record crowd watch the 1973 clash with Leeds United

A QPR A to Z | **89**

Roeder, Glenn

(1978 – 83)

Player stats:

Apps 181
Goals 18

RIGHT Glenn Roeder

GLENN ROEDER WAS 23 WHEN HE joined QPR from Orient in 1978. He'd been on loan with Notts County who had been desperate to sign him before QPR moved in with an acceptable cash offer. A centre-back of great promise, the R's paid £250,000 for Roeder, who couldn't have imagined that he'd one day lead his new club out as captain in an FA Cup final. Roeder was a stylish defender with a decent turn of pace. He often surged forward from the back and was more than useful from set-pieces. He made his debut during a 0-0 draw against Nottingham Forest but it wasn't until halfway through the 1978/79 campaign that he established himself in the team, taking the No.6 jersey on for the majority of his time at Loftus Road and scoring a respectable four goals in 28 appearances. His second season saw him finish second only to Paul Goddard in the goal-scoring stakes, netting on 10 occasions as he made a telling contribution at both ends of the park. He even invented a step-over that Hoops fans nicknamed "the Roeder Shuffle" and would use the move to initiate counter-attacks or simply get himself out of tight situations. After a steady third season at Loftus Road, Roeder, by now captain of the team, was a crucial part of Terry Venables' side and was inspirational on the R's journey to the 1982 FA Cup final. Though he skippered the side in the first

match against Spurs, he was suspended for the replay. Injury meant the contribution he made during the following year or so with QPR was limited to just 11 starts before he moved to Newcastle

United for £150,000 in December 1983. Roeder later moved into management with Gillingham, Watford, West Ham, and Newcastle. He is currently the manager of Norwich City.

ABOVE Roeder skippers the Hoops in the 1982 FA Cup final against Spurs

Rowlands, Martin

(2003 – onwards)

RIGHT
Martin Rowlands takes
the ball past Chelsea's
Claudio Pizarro

MARTIN ROWLANDS spent five years with Brentford before breaking his leg and R's boss Ian Holloway decided to bring the versatile 24-year-old to Loftus Road. QPR's financial situation dictated the players the club could bring in and more often than not, that meant a collection of bargain basement buys and free transfers – Rowlands fitted into the latter category. But, during his first season with Rangers, he played in several different positions and was excellent in all of them, though attacking midfielder was his preferred position. He bagged 12 goals, largely from midfield, and was voted Player of the Year by both the fans and his team-mates.

He also won international recognition with the Republic of Ireland, inning three caps. The Hammersmith-born player had made an instant impact, but he perhaps was too good during that first year and a succession of injuries over the next two seasons meant the popular Rowlands found it difficult to recapture that kind of form. It wasn't until he had a decent run free of problems during the 2006/07 campaign that he was back to somewhere near his best. It was only natural that he was given the captaincy for the 2007/08 campaign when he was again hugely influential for the R's and new boss Iain Dowie confirmed he was handing the armband to Rowlands once again for the 2008/09 campaign.

Seaman
(1986 – 90)

RIGHT A youthful
David Seaman, 1989

IT WAS OBVIOUS FROM THE MOment David Seaman made his debut for QPR against Southampton in 1986, that he was a special talent – despite being on the wrong end of a 5-1 hammering! While nobody would have guessed that he would go on to become one of England's most-capped players, it was clear that the £225,000 Jim Smith paid to Birmingham City for their England Under-21 keeper, was money extremely well-spent. The man who went on to become known as "Safe Hands" survived a tough first campaign in a struggling Hoops team, missing just one league match. Coached by legendary Arsenal goalkeeper Bob Wilson, Seaman improved each season and won his first full England cap against Saudi Arabia in 1988 during a 1-1 draw in Riyadh – the first of three international caps whilst with the R's. He was, however, prone to injury and averaged around 35 league games per season while at Loftus Road. His consistent displays made him a transfer target for several top clubs and in July 1990, the R's finally succumbed to Arsenal's £1.3m bid – a British record for a goalkeeper – and Seaman travelled across London to become a Highbury legend for the Gunners, winning a total of 75 caps for England, a record bettered only by Peter Shilton.

Sexton, Dave

(Manager 1974 – 77)

LIKE MANY OF THE GAME'S TOP managers, Dave Sexton had a fairly unspectacular career as a player with several non-League clubs before having spells with West Ham, Leyton Orient, Brighton and Crystal Palace. It was while at Selhurst Park that he suffered a career-ending injury and his thoughts turned towards coaching. His first job was assistant coach at Chelsea. Blessed with tactical nous and the ability to spot raw young talent, Sexton's first managerial job was with one of his former clubs, Leyton Orient, but his inexperience soon showed as the Brisbane Road outfit slumped to the foot of the division and he resigned after less than a year in the post. He returned to coaching, enjoying spells at Fulham and Arsenal before he returned to management as a replacement for Tommy Docherty at Chelsea. Sexton would replace Docherty twice during his career and his time at Stamford Bridge was hugely successful. Under his reign, the Blues won the FA Cup and European Cup Winners' Cup in

LEFT Stan Bowles, Gerry Francis, Frank McLintock and manager Dave Sexton, after QPR had beaten Leeds 2-0 to go top of the league, 1976

ABOVE Dave Sexton, 1975

FAR RIGHT Nigerian born Danny Shittu

1974. The timing was perfect with Gordon Jago having just vacated his post at Loftus Road and 13 days after leaving Chelsea, Sexton was named QPR manager. Jago had laid some sound foundations and Sexton was the perfect man to build on them. His first job was to bring in experienced midfielder Don Masson to complement the flair element of the team and Frank McLintock to help shore up the defence. The R's finished 11th at the end of the campaign and with the addition of John Hollins from Chelsea the following season, Sexton guided Rangers to their highest ever finish in the League finishing second only to Liverpool. Sexton's side played wonderful, attractive football and the mix of silk and steel saw the Hoops reach the quarter-finals of the UEFA Cup in their inaugural European campaign and the League Cup semi-finals the following season. However, Tommy Docherty's departure from yet another club – this time Manchester United – saw Sexton offered the chance to manage one of the biggest clubs in the world and, despite Rangers having thrashed the Reds 4-0 just two months earlier, he accepted the role and left Loftus Road in July 1977.

successive years (1970 and 1971) and finished runners-up in the 1972 League Cup final – quite a record. Unfortunately for Sexton, the club's ambition was greater than its bank balance and the building of a three-tier stand almost ruined Chelsea and Sexton, forcing him to sell many of his star players including Alan Hudson and Peter Osgood. As the team's fortunes dipped, Sexton was sacked in October

Shittu, Danny

(2001 – 06)

NIGERIAN POWERHOUSE DEFEN-der Danny Shittu was no ordinary purchase for QPR. The Charlton Athletic player spent two frustrating years at The Valley and was loaned out to Blackpool before manager Ian Holloway brought the strapping centre-back to Loftus Road on loan in October 2001. Holloway liked what he saw immediately, but the club hadn't got the money needed to fund a permanent deal – until wealthy Rangers fans Matt and Alex Winton came forward to finance an estimated £350,000 deal during the January 2002 transfer win-dow – to pay Shittu's wages for the first year! "Big Dan", already a Nigeria international, became an instant hit with the R's supporters with his no-nonsense style and he cut a mean figure too, weighing more than 15 stone and standing at 6' 3". A constant threat from set-pieces, Shittu's reputation as one of the best defenders outside the Premier League grew stronger each season. After four years at Loftus Road, it became clear that the player had ambitions to

Player stats:

Apps 162
Goals 17

SHITTU

FAR RIGHT
Trevor Sinclair, 1995

BELOW Danny Shittu celebrates scoring with his team-mates

play in the top-flight and when West Brom agreed a fee of £1.6m, Shittu underwent a medical for the Baggies – but Watford manager Aidy Boothroyd's late call convinced the Super Eagle to instead sign for the Hornets. In 2008 he joined Bolton Wanderers for £2m but for Rangers fans, he remains one of the

most popular players to have represented QPR in the last decade, hence the following song:

Chim chimeny, Chim chimeny
Chim, chim, cher-oo
Who needs Sol Campbell
When we've got Shittu?

Sinclair, Trevor

(1993 – 98)

TREVOR SINCLAIR BOMBING DOWN the right flank with his trademark dreadlock hairstyle was a familiar sight to QPR fans during the 1990s. The dashing winger joined Rangers from Blackpool in 1993 for £600,000 as a replacement for Sheffield Wednesday-bound Andy Sinton and was an instant hit with the Loftus Road faithful. Brought to the club by Gerry Francis, Sinclair settled into his new surrounds quickly and provided a number of assists for Les Ferdinand during his first two seasons, though his own scoring ratio was not perhaps what it should have been and he averaged just four a season with the Hoops. When he did find the net, however, it was invariably a screamer and when Rangers took on Barnsley during an FA Cup tie in 1997, Sinclair's spectacular bicycle kick from 20 yards out was one of the greatest goals ever witnessed at Loftus Road and was voted Goal of the Season for 1996/97 on Match of the Day. He won England Under-21 caps and played for England B team during his time with

Player stats:

Apps	186 + 5 sub
Goals	21

ABOVE Trevor Sinclair, 1995

FAR RIGHT
Andy Sinton playing
for England

the Hoops but it wasn't until his surprise move across London to West Ham that he won full England honours. The Hammers paid £2.3m for Sinclair in January 1998 and he later joined his boyhood favourites Manchester City and later Cardiff City before being released by the Bluebirds in 2008.

Sinton, Andy
(1989 – 93)

ANDY SINTON WAS A SPEEDY winger who more than repaid the faith the club had shown in signing him. Having played in the lower leagues with Cambridge and Brentford, Sinton was regularly watched by other clubs but it was Trevor Francis who gambled on the 23-year-old with the Super Hoops paying the Bees £300,000 for the player in March 1989. Sinton made an instant impression during his debut two days later – a 2-0 win at Sheffield Wednesday and he scored the winning goal on his home debut against Aston Villa two days after that – quite a start! Sinton added a new dynamic to the flanks – supplying chances for "Sir" Les Ferdinand and was soon selected for the England B team. He was an ever-present during his first full season and in November 1991 he won his first full cap for England. He would go on to become a regular for his country over the next few years. Versatile in that he could switch wings or play in midfield – and even played full-back for England on one occasion – Sinton's time with QPR

Player stats:

Apps 191
Goals 25

was enjoyable for both the fans and the player. He scored the opening goal in the famous 4-1 win at Manchester United and he also scored Rangers' first Premiership goal – a cracking effort away to Manchester City during Sky Sports' first Monday night live match.

He left Loftus Road a much better player and his £2.75m move to Sheffield Wednesday helped the club's bank balance no end. He later played for Spurs and Wolves before moving into management in non-League football.

RIGHT Sinton skips past Spurs' Paul Allen

Smith, Jim
(Manager 1985 – 88)

JIM SMITH – "THE BALD EAGLE" – arrived at Loftus Road following the departure of Alan Mullery and following a brief spell as caretaker by Frank Sibley. Having taken Oxford United into the top-flight for the first time in the club's history, Smith's stock was high and his time at Loftus Road was fairly successful. In his first campaign he guided the R's to a 6-0 win over Chelsea and also took the Hoops to the 1986 League Cup final at Wembley having seen off Chelsea, Nottingham Forest and Liverpool along the way. In one of football's many ironies, Rangers took on Smith's old club Oxford in the final, but lost 3-0 after a disappointing performance. The 1986/87 season saw a number of heavy defeat's for the R's including three 4-1 hammerings, a 5-1 reverse at Southampton on the opening day (!) and a 7-1 loss at Sheffield Wednesday. The board kept faith with Smith and were rewarded by a much better season in 1987/88. The R's topped the table for several weeks after a blistering start to the campaign with eight victories from

ABOVE Jim Smith with the Oxford United Manager Maurice Evans, 1986

their opening 10 games, but just one win in the next 10 undid much of the good work. Rangers eventually finished in fifth and were London's top-placed club, but when chairman David Bulstrode died suddenly not long into the following campaign, Smith decided to leave Loftus Road and took over as manager of Newcastle United.

Stainrod, Simon

(1980 – 85)

Player stats:

Apps 175 + 2 sub

Goals 62

RIGHT The silky-skilled Simon Stainrod

AVERAGING A GOAL EVERY THREE games during his time with the Super Hoops, Simon Stainrod was just 21 when he joined from Oldham Athletic in November 1980. The silky-skilled striker began his career with home-town club Sheffield United. He was a natural Rangers No.10 and he donned the coveted jersey on his debut at Preston North End and wasted no time settling in at Loftus Road with three goals in his next six games. Stainrod was a delight to watch and possessed superb control and technique and he became a pivotal part of Terry Venables' side play-ing 52 matches during his first full sea-son in 1981/82, scoring 24 goals. He played in both FA Cup final matches against Tottenham and was hugely impressive again during the 1982/83 campaign, scoring nine goals as the Hoops won promotion back to the top-flight. Hugely popular on the terraces, Stainrod's style and panache were exactly what the R's fans craved and he scored 16 goals in his third campaign with the club. When the influential Venables left for Barcelona in 1984, Alan Mullery took over and gradually, a talented side began to fall apart. In November 1985, almost five years to the day since he'd signed, Stainrod moved to his boyhood heroes Sheffield Wednesday for £250,000. He later played for Aston Villa and Stoke before playing for French sides Strasbourg and FC Rouen. He returned to play for Falkirk and Ayr United and dabbled in management with Dundee for a spell. Stainrod is today based in Cannes as a FIFA-licensed football agent.

Stejskal, Jan

(1990 – 94)

THOUGH TONY ROBERTS HAD proved a reliable understudy to David Seaman during his time with the club, Don Howe was keen to bring a proven international keeper in to replace the Highbury-bound Seaman and so turned to Czechoslovakia's No.1 custodian Jan Stejskal. The 28-year-old Stejskal had been at Sparta Praha for seven years and spoke little English. He made his league debut for the R's against Leeds United in October 1990, a game in which Rangers came from 2-0 down to win 3-2. Stejskal had been at fault for both Leeds goals, setting the tone for what proved to be a rocky first year in England. Living in a foreign country, apart from his family and still unable to communicate satisfactorily with his team-mates, Stejskal was finding the pace and style of English football difficult to adjust to and he made a number of unforced errors resulting in some of the Rangers fans calling for him to be replaced by Roberts. But the Czech star dug in, worked hard and gradually won over the doubters with a sustained period of superb displays. Back with his family and more comfortable with the language, Stejskal then had the added bonus of being coached by Hoops legend Phil Parkes and his popularity continued to rise steadily with his sometimes almost super-human displays. Standing at 6' 7", Stejskal cut a commanding figure in his goal and had great agility for such a tall man. By the time he left to join Slavia Prague in 1994, he'd become one of the most popular overseas players to have ever played for the club and certainly one of the best keepers Loftus Road has seen in the last 20 years.

Player stats:

Apps 107
Goals 0

BELOW A determined looking Stejskal

Stock, Alec

(1937 – 39)

& Manager (1959 – 68)

ALEC STOCK'S CAREER AS A PLAYER was cut short by the Second World War and he made just 28 official appearances, though added another 28 during wartime games for Rangers. A natural leader, he rose to the rank of major in the Royal Armoured Corps and was badly injured in action in 1944. He later became player-manager of Yeovil Town, guiding the Somerset outfit to an incredible FA Cup victory over Sunderland in 1949. He would manage Leyton Orient and AS Roma, as well as having a brief spell as assistant manager at Arsenal. He finally found his way back to Loftus Road in 1959 and was given the task of rebuilding QPR into a major force. Stock laid the club's foundations by setting up an excellent youth policy and with the backing of new chairman Jim Gregory, bought the likes of Brian Bedford, Mark Lazarus and Rodney Marsh in for prudent transfer fees. Stock introduced youngsters such as the Morgan twins into the team and the club went from strength to strength, culminating in the unforgettable 1966/67 season when Rangers were promoted to Division Two as well as winning the League Cup. Stock proved what a superb manager he was the following campaign when his Rangers side achieved back-to-back promotions to take their place in the top-flight for the first time. Sadly, despite all his success, there was increased expectation and unwanted pressure from within the club due to his health problems, encouraged Stock to resign and he never managed the R's in Division One. Stock's departure left a huge void at Loftus Road and his replacement, Tommy Docherty, was fired after just 28 days! The club finished bottom of the table in their first season without him. After productive periods with Luton Town and Fulham (whom he took to the 1975 FA Cup final as a Third Division side), Stock returned to QPR as a director and even became caretaker boss over the summer of 1978 before moving on to Bournemouth. A visionary who was way ahead of his time, Alec Stock passed away in 2001. He remains the most successful manager the club has ever had and most importantly, he did it in style and put Queens Park Rangers on the football map forever.

Thomas, Dave
(1972 – 77)

QPR BOSS GORDON JAGO MADE A number of fine acquisitions during his three-year tenure at Loftus Road, and most would agree that Dave Thomas was one of the best. The tricky, versatile winger was a genuine threat wherever he played and that Jago convinced promotion rivals Burnley to part with their prized asset for a fee of £165,000 is amazing. Thomas signed in October 1972 and strengthened an attack that already included Stan Bowles and Don Givens. He made his debut in a 3-2 win over Sunderland and managed half-a-dozen strikes during a season which saw Rangers win promotion back to Division One, ironically one point behind champions Burnley! Thomas had electric pace but his main asset was his superb crossing and he could whip inviting balls across all day long, given the space and service. Thomas was rarely injured and missed just one game for three successive years. He won his first England cap against Czechoslovakia in 1974 – one of eight caps he won while with Rangers. He played 44 times for the R's in his final season at Loftus Road before moving to Everton in a £200,000 deal.

Player stats:

Apps	219 + 1sub
Goals	33

LEFT Dave Thomas

Underdogs

FEW QPR FANS ENTERTAINED thoughts of Wembley when the then Third Division R's were drawn at home to Colchester United. Playing under floodlights competitively for the first time, Sir Stanley Rous switched on the Loftus Road floodlights and Rodney Marsh illuminated the crowd with a four-goal salvo against the Essex side. Mark Lazarus was the other scorer in a 5-0 romp watched by 5,497 people. Aldershot provided stiffer opposition in the second round, holding Rangers to a 1-1 draw on their own patch before

bowing out to two late goals at Loftus Road in the replay. Swansea arrived in Shepherds Bush for round three having played a league game at Loftus Road just four days earlier. The Welsh side took the lead, but an own goal and a last minute winner from Mike Keen put Alec Stock's side into the last 16 where they were drawn at home to First Division Leicester. The Foxes, with England goalkeeper Gordon Banks among their number, fell behind to a Roger Morgan goal, but a brace from Derek Dougan gave the visitors the lead at the break.

The 20,000-plus Rangers fans roared their team on and were rewarded with an equaliser on 56 minutes when Les Allen's shot bounced off the bar and in off Banks and the Hoops then added another two in the next four minutes to send the Loft wild with delight to complete a 4-2 win. With yet another home tie, this time against Second Division pace-setters Carlisle in the quarter-final, Rangers began to believe the impossible

ABOVE
John Byrne evades Liverpool defender Alan Hansen

FAR LEFT QPR in action against West Bromwich Albion during the League Cup Final at Wembley, 1967

RIGHT Trevor Hebberd
of Oxford tackles
Gary Bannister

might be possible – even more so after Marsh's double strike won the game 2-1 to send the club into the semi-finals. Only First Division Birmingham City stood between the R's and a Wembley cup final and at a packed St Andrew's in the first leg, it seemed as though the Blues might prove one hurdle too many for Stock's excellent side. Falling behind to a fourth-minute goal, Blues fans settled back to enjoy a goal-feast – and that's exactly what they got, only they were all scored by QPR who rattled in four second half strikes to win 4-1. It was a magnificent effort, worthy of a Wembley appearance, yet Stock ensured his players remained professional during the second leg – which they did – and a 3-1 win was no more than Rangers deserved. Rodney Marsh had proved inspirational throughout the run with 10 goals and his reward was a stage fit for him to show the rest of the country what a talent he was. First Division West Brom awaited Stock's heroes in the final, watched by a record crowd of 97,952 but the R's started nervously and went into the break fortunate to be just 2-0 down. With an hour gone, it seemed as though the dream was over, but when Roger

Morgan pulled it back to 2-1 on 63 minutes, the QPR players seemed to grow in stature and belief. It would take something special to bring them back on level terms – and that's exactly what happened, with Rodney Marsh scoring the goal of his life after a mazy dribble ended with a clinical finish. Wembley went wild – well, at least half of it. The drama wasn't quite over as Albion almost re-took the lead, but the script called for a Rangers winner and nine minutes from the end, Lazarus rolled the ball home to make it 3-2. QPR had truly arrived and it had taken a monumental effort from a gifted group of players to land the club's first major trophy.

The R's love affair with the League Cup continued with a second appearance in the final in 1986, though on this occasion the R's were anything but underdogs. Having seen off Hull City 8-1 on aggregate over two legs, Watford 1-0, Nottingham Forest 3-1 and Chelsea at Stamford Bridge, Jim Smith's side faced Liverpool in a two legged semi-final. A hard-fought 1-0 victory over the Reds gave the R's a slight advantage going into the second leg at Anfield. Liverpool's Steve McMahon levelled the aggregate in the first half and Jan Molby had the chance to make it 2-0 from the spot just before the break – but acting on advice from former Reds' striker Mike Robinson, now with Rangers, Paul Barron saved the kick. After the break a comical own goal from Ronnie Whelan gave the R's the edge again but back came Liverpool with a second 12 minutes later through Craig Johnston. It was to be the visitor's night, with yet another own goal sending Smith's side to Wembley for only the third major final in Rangers' history, though their second in just four years against Jim Smith's former club Oxford United. Having drawn 3-3 in the league just a month earlier, the 90,000-plus crowd were hopeful of another end-to-end encounter, but the QPR fans were left feeling flat as the Hoops never really got to grips with a hard-working Oxford side that ran out comfortable 3-0 winners on the day.

Venables, Terry
(1969 – 74)
& Manager (1980 – 84)

THERE WERE TWO CAREERS FOR Terry Venables at QPR – one as a creative midfielder and the other as one of the brightest young managers in the country. Venables began his career with Chelsea before moving on to Spurs and enjoyed great success with both clubs, winning England recognition along the way. He arrived at Loftus Road in 1969, shortly after the R's had been relegated from the First Division as Les Allen attempted to rebuild a side whose confidence had been shattered during the disastrous campaign in the top-flight. Venables often wore the No.4 jersey and he had an impressive first season with the Super Hoops, playing 42 times and scoring seven goals. His second year with the club was even more successful as he found the net 11 times in 40 starts, winning himself a sizeable fan club in the process. He led the R's back to Division One by skippering the team during the 1972/73 season and he transferred to the fourth London club in September 1974 having become a hugely popular figure during his time at Loftus Road. Just six years later, the enigmatic Venables returned to manage the Hoops – then in Division Two – and within two years had guided QPR to a first ever FA Cup final against one

Player stats:

Apps	205 + 1 sub
Goals	22

LEFT Terry Venables, 1971

of his former clubs Spurs. It was a remarkable achievement by a manager who liked his teams to play with style and flair, but was clearly something of a tactical genius. In his third campaign as manager, Venables took Rangers back into the top division after winning Division Two by 10 points and his talented side finished the 1983/84 season just one league win off second place. Undoubtedly the hottest property in English management, it was no surprise when Barcelona came calling for his service – an offer that was too good to turn down and the man who'd done so much for QPR left his post bound for the Nou Camp. Later in his career he would manage England and came within a penalty shoot-out of steering the nation to the 1996 European Championship final.

Webb, David
(1974 – 77)

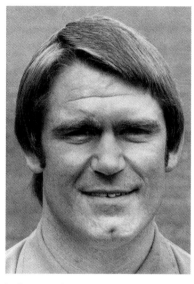

Player stats:

Apps	146+
	1 sub
Goals	11

DAVID WEBB, THE MAN WHO once scored the winning goal in the 1970 FA Cup final, was one of a batch of experienced pros brought to the club by Dave Sexton. Rangers bought the no-nonsense defender from Chelsea for £120,000 and the 28-year-old Webb slotted straight into central defence and would adopt the No.6 jersey for all but four of his 147 appearances for the R's. Webb made his debut against Sheffield United on August 16 and made 39 appearances during his first campaign. Webb's nous and organisational skills played a huge part in Rangers' superb 1975/76 season with his enthusiasm and total commitment to the Hoops' cause winning him a legion of fans at Loftus Road. Like many great players before – and since – Webb would probably count his penalty miss against AEK Athens in the shoot-out for a place in the UEFA Cup semi-final as one of his career lows, but he wasn't about to sit around and dwell on his failure and was back to his inspirational best for the remainder of the 1976/77 season. He gave his all right up until his final game for the club – ironically against Chelsea in September 1977 – after which he joined Leicester City for £50,000.

Wegerle, Roy

(1989 – 92)

SOUTH AFRICAN-BORN STRIKER Roy Wegerle was one of those maverick strikers that simply had to play for QPR at some point in his career. His path to Loftus Road was a complicated one, initially starting life in South African football before having an unsuccessful trial with Manchester United. After a spell in the NASL with Tampa Bay Rowdies – during which time he was coached by Rangers legend Rodney Marsh – he moved to indoor soccer league outfit Tacoma Stars for a further two years. He returned to England after Marsh convinced Jim Smith to give him a trial with the Hoops, but it was Chelsea who paid £100,000 to secure his services. His time with the Blues was patchy at best and he was loaned to Swindon Town before joining Luton Town for £75,000. Almost 18 months later, his value had rocketed and new Rangers boss Don Howe's first act was to purchase Wegerle for a cool £1m. It was a lot of money to pay for a player who'd had a nomadic career up until then but Howe was convinced Wegerle was the magical No.10

the club needed. A precocious talent, Wegerle repaid Howe's faith by finishing top scorer in his first full season at the club, starting the 1990/91 campaign with nine goals in the first 10 matches. His penchant for spectacular goals had the supporters eating out of the palm of his hand and one of his two strikes away to Leeds United in October 1990 won ITV's Goal of the Season award. He was the archetypal No.10, all flair and grace but not much in the way of hard work and when Blackburn Rovers offered not only to give Rangers their money back – plus a bit more – for the talismanic forward in March 1992, new manager Gerry Francis was happy to accept. Wegerle continued to wander from club to club, finishing his playing career in the USA.

BELOW Roy Wegerle

Player stats:

Apps 89 + 4 sub
Goals 31

X-tra time

RIGHT QPR players
with Ian Holloway
celebrate victory

QPR'S ONLY EXPERIENCE OF THE Football League play-offs is, unfortunately, an unhappy one. During a steady 2002/03 campaign under manager Ian Holloway, the Hoops finished in fourth place, meaning a play-off semi-final against fifth placed Oldham Athletic with the winners facing either Bristol City or Cardiff City at the Millennium Stadium in the final. Oldham were managed by former Rangers player Iain Dowie and the first leg was played at Boundary Park. The Latics opened the scoring early on but Richard Langley equalised after the break to give Ollie's side a slight advantage. In one of the most atmospheric nights at Loftus Road for many years, it was the club's "Rolls Royce", Paul Furlong, who smoothly tucked home a late winner to send the home fans wild and win the

game 1-0. Cardiff had edged past Bristol City meaning the final would be played in their own backyard. With a packed crowd of 66,096 watching and 30,000 Rangers fans roaring the team on, it was the R's who looked the better team for most of the game, but with no goals scored in normal time, the match went into extra time for another nerve-wracking 30 minutes. With the match seemingly heading for penalties, Cardiff sub Andy Campbell broke through to score what proved to be the winning goal four minutes from time. It was heartbreaking stuff, but Rangers would come back stronger the following season and win promotion automatically on the final day of the 2003/04 campaign – without the need for the dreaded extra time!

Youngest

FRANK SIBLEY, A LOYAL CLUB servant who played, coached and managed the R's over three decades' worth of wonderful service, also holds the record as QPR's youngest-ever player. Aged 15 years and nine months exactly, Sibley made his debut against Aldershot during a 3-1 League Cup defeat in September 1963. Sibley played three more times in the league during the 1963/64 campaign, by then at the grand old age of 16, but few who saw the teenager at that point would have envisaged he would become part of the fabric of the club in the manner he eventually did. Sibley's playing career was cut short by injury and he was forced to retire aged only 24. Having played 168 times for the club, he then moved onto the coaching staff at Loftus Road and when Dave Sexton left the

Hoops for Manchester United in 1977, the Rangers board made Sibley the new manager. However, the club struggled under Sibley who guided the team to just nine wins in 45 games. He resigned after a year in charge, but returned to the club as reserve team manager in 1984 and when Terry Venables left to manage Barcelona, Sibley was again asked to manage the club, this time in the role of caretaker boss from December 1984 until the end of the season. Sibley returned to coaching duties thereafter with Alan Mullery taking on the job. Sibley's managerial record of just 17 wins in 73 games meant he was never offered the role again, probably to his great relief!

Zenith Data Systems

THE ILL-FATED (AND UNFORTU-nately named) Zenith Data Systems (ZDS) Cup lasted just three seasons before being consigned to the history books as nothing more than annoyance. The paying public had little interest in a competition that it seemed most clubs treated with complete disdain – there was no TV coverage, no European reward for the team that actually won the competition and only a run to the final itself would generate any worthwhile income. Previously known as the Full Member's Cup and the Simod Cup, Rangers played just three games in the ZDS. On November 20, 1990, the R's were in the middle of an appalling run of defeats in the league, so a trip to face a Southampton side that had beaten Rangers 3-1 just 10 days earlier was hardly what the doctor ordered. The handful of QPR fans that made the journey to The Dell returned to West London even more miserable than when they'd set off as the Saints inflicted a merciless 4-0 hammering which was smack in the middle of a nine-game losing streak. The following season, Rangers recorded a 2-1 win at Norwich City thanks to goals from Andy Sinton and Andy Impey before losing 3-2 at Loftus Road to Crystal Palace in front of a meagre 4,492 fans – David Bardsley and Ray Wilkins scoring the R's goals on the night.

Other books also available:

 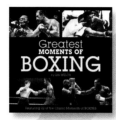 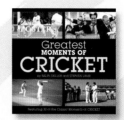 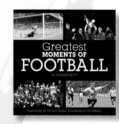

  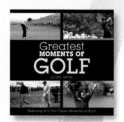 

Available from all major stockists

LITTLE BOOK OF THE
OLYMPICS
AN OLYMPIC A to Z
Written by Jon Stroud

THE LITTLE BOOK OF
HORSERACING
A HORSERACING A to Z
Written by James Whittaker and Clive Youlton

The Little Book of
CRICKET
LEGENDS
ANDY DELLOR and LIONEL LAMB

The Little Book of
GOLF
LEGENDS
NICK TAPPIN

The Little Book of
FOOTBALL
LEGENDS
GRAHAM BETTS

The Little Book of
RUGBY
LEGENDS
WILL MORGAN and ALEX MEAD

The Little Book of
GRAND PRIX
LEGENDS
PHILIP RABY

THE LITTLE BOOK OF
EUROPEAN FOOTBALL
Written by Graham Betts

THE LITTLE BOOK OF
FISHING
Angler's Mail
A FISHING A to Z
Written by Rob Yarko

THE LITTLE BOOK OF
JANE AUSTEN

LITTLE BOOK OF THE
BRONTË SISTERS

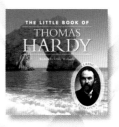
THE LITTLE BOOK OF
THOMAS HARDY

Available from all major stockists

The pictures in this book were provided courtesy of the following:

GETTY IMAGES
101 Bayham Street, London NW1 0AG

PA PHOTOS
PA Photos.com

Design and artwork by Jane Stephens

Creative Director Kevin Gardner

Image research by Ellie Charleston

Published by Green Umbrella Publishing

Publishers Jules Gammond, Vanessa Gardner

Written by David Clayton